RELENTLESS
PARENTING

THE CRUCIAL PURSUIT OF YOUR TEEN'S HEART

By Brian and Angela Haynes

randall house
114 Bush Rd | Nashville, TN 37217 | randallhouse.com

Published by Randall House Publications
114 Bush Road
Nashville, TN 37217

Printed in the United States of America

ISBN-13: 9780892659890

To Hailey, Madelyn, and Eden. We love you.

To the parents raising the young men that will marry our daughters some day…

SH'MA! (Dt. 6:4-7)

Acknowledgments

Several years ago, when we began leading churches to think about making disciples by equipping families, we never dreamed that God would allow us to influence people beyond our own home and our own church. We are humbled and grateful that Jesus would choose to use us to communicate anything on His behalf. Particularly a message as important as one bent on turning the hearts of parents toward their children, and the hearts of children to their parents. We acknowledge, Jesus, the King of Kings and Lord of Lords. He is the Alpha and the Omega; the beginning and the end. He is the victorious Lamb of God who takes away sin and reverses its monstrous effects. He is the Good Shepherd who keeps His covenant of love to a thousand generations of those who love Him and keep His commands. It is by you and for you, Jesus.

We want to say thank you to Saundra Hardesty and Katy Buckaloo for their tireless support in this project. Thanks, once again, to Francis Knox for opening her home in Jamaica Beach, Texas, to us as a writing getaway. Thanks to Randall House and the D6 family, particularly Michelle Orr and Ron Hunter, for believing in our message. I pray the world is becoming a different place because of our collaboration ... one home at a time.

Table of Contents

Preface

Our story to this point is one of imperfection and extravagant grace. This is now the third book in the area of family ministry and parenting that we have written. I say "we" because, even though the first two books have my name on them only, Angela was a source of wisdom, a partner in parenting, and personally sacrificial so that I could write and speak with churches and families about equipping strategies for leading children spiritually. The first book, *Shift: What it Takes to Finally Reach Families Today* (2009), was birthed out of our personal struggle to learn how to lead our children biblically. As we developed a plan, it developed for the church in ways that we could not have imagined back then.

Chapter one of that book started like this: "I'll never forget it as long as I live. I packed up her new pink backpack, tied her shoes, and strapped her into the car seat to take her to school. It was the first day of Kindergarten and Hailey, my oldest daughter, was ready to go. I, on the other hand, was a total mess."[1] Since that day a lot of water has gone under the bridge, so to speak. We now have two teenagers, and another one not far behind, living in our house. More recently, we sat at Whataburger®, God's "fast food hamburger" gift to Texas, and watched our daughter who we once strapped into the car seat, drive off on her own. We reminisced about the Kindergarten drop off and laughed. What a crazy, imperfect, stressful, grace-filled, relentless, joyous journey, is this thing called parenting. Man! It never stops and the experience seems to change moment by moment.

The teen years are especially challenging but also incredibly great, no doubt about it. We are living it. We have been parenting at least one teenager for about five years now. If my calculations are correct and if the Lord is willing, we will be parenting at least one teenager for the next eleven years. As you can imagine we are now around a lot of teens and their families. Many of our best friends are parents of adolescents. Add to that our work in the local church and in family ministry and you could say we hear from tons of parents of teenagers.

We have noticed a trend that, while understandable, is sad to us. So many parents of teenagers seem frustrated, even verbalizing a level of disdain and disconnection with their adolescent children. More than once we have heard parents of teenagers say things like, "Now I know why animals eat their young" or "I can't wait for them to leave home." Often these sentiments are coupled with relational disconnection because it is easier to be distant than to relentlessly engage with this age group. Maybe you have had similar thoughts or even feel contempt and withdrawal from your own children. Maybe you are tempted to take the easy road when it comes to parenting your teen by avoiding the conflict that often comes with leading them. It is very possible that you feel hopeless when it comes to your teenager. Or, you may just feel like you need some practical help navigating a new season of parenting. All of this is totally understandable. We have felt it, thought it, and lived it. And...we still are. We are sojourners and, like you, we need others to encourage us to be relentless in the pursuit of our teenagers' hearts.

We have made an attempt in this book to be as honest and as transparent as possible without dishonoring our children. We have their permission to share everything you will read. We think it is in our openness that you will best learn to relentlessly love your teenager. Rest assured, as you are reading this, we have prayed for you—not by name but in general. We have prayed for every parent that God allows to read this book. May the Lord grant you much hope and joy in the relationship you have with your child that is becoming an adult. May He grant you wisdom beyond yourself to know what to do when you don't know what to do. May God guide your steps as you lead your teenagers biblically. May the Lord connect your heart with your teenager's heart as you relentlessly pursue him, especially when you don't feel like it. You are not alone, friend. Be relentless. It is crucial.

Endnotes

[1] Brian Haynes, *Shift: What it Takes to Finally Reach Families Today* (Loveland, CO: Group Publishing, 2009), 27.

But he said to me, "My grace is sufficient for you, for my power is made perfect in weakness." Therefore I will boast all the more gladly of my weaknesses, so that the power of Christ may rest upon me. For the sake of Christ, then, I am content with weaknesses, insults, hardships, persecutions, and calamities. For when I am weak, then I am strong.

—2 Corinthians 12:9-10

Chapter 1

Who Your Teenagers Are ... and Who They Are Not

Let's start here. We are not experts, though for some reason God has given us a voice with other parents. Like you, we are on a journey. Our prayer is that at the end of our lives as we look back we will observe a legacy of faith spanning the generations that will flow from our family of five. We are not there yet. It's not time to look back. It's too soon to declare victory. We are in the midst of the most joyous, gut wrenching, grace covered, adventure and love story called parenting; and we have teenagers. Each child is completely unique and each is a blessing in her own way. We would not trade any of them. We are madly in love with our kids. Daily we are learning what it means to parent them toward adulthood. We've never done this before and because of our imperfection and inexperience and truthfully our sin, it's not easy. What was God thinking when he made forty-something sinners the parents of teenage sinners? Yet, we count this journey as undeniably the most amazing experience of our lifetime and we are thankful. We are compelled to be faithful because of our love for God and our love for the children He gave us. I bet the same goes for you.

Parenting teenagers is different than parenting younger children. It's funny how right before our eyes in a very short time, four-year-olds become fourteen. Though we can see the four-year-olds when we look into their eyes, at fourteen they have changed drastically in every way: physically, biological-ly, emotionally, and spiritually. They think their own thoughts, have their own dreams, and are beginning to live their own way under the covering of, you guessed it, their parents. This is no time to check out. We have to understand who our teenagers are and how they are different from the little ones we have been parenting for so long. We also need to clearly understand who they are not ... or at least not yet.

Who is my teenager?

I can think of several times as a father, that I have been shocked by who my teenagers are becoming. Sometimes in my mind they are still seven. Recently I was at an event for church and I was looking for one of our daughters. I scanned the room three or four different times. I looked near. I looked far. And then I finally asked someone if they had seen her. They pointed to a table where Angela was sitting and there with her back to me sat a beautiful young woman—my daughter. I missed her three or so times because I was looking for my little girl. For many parents this kind of epiphany elicits fear. However, we must walk in faith seeking to understand who that teenager is despite the season of life.

Foundationally we must understand that our teenagers were created by God and like all of humanity, they are His children. When you look into the face of your teenager whether it is a good or bad day, keep this in mind, "So God created man in his own image, in the image of God he created him; male and female he created them."[1] Your teenager was created in the image of God. If you espouse a biblical worldview, this is where we begin in parenting at any season. Certain implications arise from this pivotal understanding. If God created our children then by nature, He knows them best. He knows all about their spiritual, physical, and emotional reality. He understands the thoughts of their minds, the meditations of their hearts, and the root associated with the words of their mouths. God is their designer and their perfect Father. He knows what they need, when they need it, and how they need it. The good news is He is also your designer. He knows what wisdom you need, when you need it, and how you need it. He is a perfect Father when our parenting skills seem grossly inadequate. He knows when you need grace, patience, endurance, and compassion. He knows when you are angry—when that anger is righteous and when it is not. He is your counselor and source. This is an amazing, supernatural source of hope and comfort. Remember, God chose you as a parent to steward His creation (that teenager you call your own), which is a blessing. Understanding that they are His creation is fundamental. Realizing they were created in His image is sometimes baffling. In the good moments it's easy to glimpse the handiwork of God. If you are like us, in the rough moments all you can see is your own image making for a potentially upsetting and convicting experience. This is when it is important to remember whose creation we are stewarding.

God, as a perfect Father, did not just create our teenagers in His own image and then walk away. Instead He created each of them with a distinct sense of uniqueness for His glory. Psalm 139:13-16 says, "For you formed my inward parts; you knitted me together in my mother's womb. I praise you, for I am fearfully and wonderfully made. Wonderful are your works; my soul knows it very well. My frame was not hidden from you, when I was being made in secret, intricately woven in the depths of the earth. Your eyes saw my unformed substance; in your book were written, every one of them, the days that were formed for me, when as yet there was none of them."[2]

From the moment of conception, God began weaving together the heart, mind, soul, and bodies of our now teenaged children for a greater reason than just blessing us as parents. He has a purpose and a plan for them that when lived out, mysteriously colors in a part of the grand mosaic of creation, bringing glory to God throughout the generations. The unique nature of each child requires personalities, skill sets, passions, and dreams that might be altogether different than those of dear old Mom and Dad. As children become teenagers, personalities, bents, and desires begin to emerge and should be honed. God uses parents and the family of origin among countless other experiences like church, relationships, and environment to shape children into the men or women He designed them to become for His glory. Think about this with a great sense of hope. Our teenagers are created precisely by God to accomplish His purpose. That principle is easy to see on the "proud, teary-eyed, look at my baby" mountaintops. The axiom is equally true in the "depressive, fearful, throw up in a trash can" moments. Here is your handhold when you feel like you are hanging off the sheer cliff of parenting teenagers: God created your teenager in His image with uniqueness to accomplish His purposes. This is what we build on, hope in, and lead toward as parents of teenagers. It is just so easy to lose sight of who they are in the craziness of parenting them.

It is helpful as parents to comprehend the general aspects of teenage development. If you are parenting a teenager, we assume that you understand your teenager's body is rapidly changing. We're sure that you regularly observe the realities of raging hormones, but there may be some things going on that you have not thought about. We hope to alleviate some parental confusion or even frustration with this information. In an article titled, "The Teen Brain is Still Under Construction," the National Institute of Mental Health reports on research findings related to the brain development of teenagers. They draw some simple yet enlightening conclusions. In many ways the brain does not look like that of an adult until the early twenties. It's interesting; a teenager may be at their lifelong pinnacle related to physical health and strength, yet the brain is still developing. It may not be surprising to understand that, "The most basic functions (of the brain) mature first: those involved, for example, in the processing of information from the senses, and in controlling movement. The parts of the brain responsible for more 'top down' control, controlling impulses, and planning ahead—the hallmarks of adult behavior—are among the last to mature."[3] At the same time, hormones are raging—impacting the brain's response to stress. Our conclusions and experience: while the teenager is at peak learning capacity, they are often unable to adequately process emotions experiencing some level of impulsiveness. They definitely are not yet able to cope with stress as an emotionally healthy adult. This little tidbit of research tells you that you are not alone when parenting an emotional or impulsive teenager.

Interestingly enough, Christian thinkers suggest this late brain development has a lot to do with environment. Dr. Richard Ross of Southwestern Baptist Theological Seminary and a leading expert in the development of teenagers reminds us that, "At seventeen, your great-grandfather likely plowed all day behind a mule and then went home to help with the baby. Your great-grandmother worked just as hard and just as competently. At sixteen she washed clothes by hand with soap she made, cooked from a fire she built, roasted chickens she raised herself, took care of the children, planted her own garden, and still had time to care for her husband. Both performed well in their roles because adults had invested years preparing them for just that."[4] How many times have you heard the phrase, "Kids these days ..." uttered in a frustrated, sarcastic tone in observance of the youth culture. It is likely true that "kids these days" just like "kids back in the day" are a product of their environmental and cultural journey. As parents we influence that.

The prevailing research suggests that the brain constantly develops and remaps throughout life not only according to biology and physiology but also according to experience. "That is, what we choose to experience, where we choose to place our attention, shapes the structure and functions of our own brains. This shaping continues following the choices that we make as long as we live."[5] This is an important concept for every parent of an adolescent to understand. Though their brain may not be fully developed—explaining impulsivity, experiences during the elementary and teenage years actually matter to brain development. It is why our forefathers functioned as adults in the teen years. They were trained for it in model and experience, shaping their brains. It is good to know that as a parent you can demonstrate a way of living and afford the child experiences that will influence the development of their brain.

Not only that, either in a positive or negative way, what a teenager thinks about regularly or dwells on also affects the brain. "What we give our focused attention to—to this action and not that one, to this attitude and not that one, to this thought and not that one—changes the actual structure and wiring of our brains for as long as we live."[6] This is also good news for the parent. Hopefully, early in childhood parents can begin to focus the attention of their children on the person of Christ, the truth of His Word, the importance of living His way, and the gravity of His mission. Even if they do not start this at an early age, the parent in partnership with the faith community has the opportunity to focus teenagers this way and it's not really that difficult. It is easily observable that teenagers are searching for a cause to live for that will out-live them. There is nothing quite as compelling as the thought of taking the saving message of Jesus Christ to every man, woman, and child, offering a message that will change the eternal destiny of a person. What they are consumed with will consume them, for a lifetime.

We have chosen to involve our children in the mission of Christ as teenagers because we have seen with our own eyes how serving the world with the gospel whether it be on your street or on the other side of the planet, impacts the way of a teenager, for life.

Years ago, Angela and I served in a local church as youth pastor and youth leader. We had the opportunity to involve dozens of teenagers in local, national, and international short-term mission experiences. We saw firsthand how leading teenagers to be on mission with Christ in a short-term way impacts their ability to walk with Christ every day. This is largely due to the ability of Jesus to consume the mind of a teenager, leading them to meditate on His words and live according to His mission. Experiencing that with the children of others later influenced us. Now as parents of teenagers, we give our teens these experiences. We have served side by side with our children in our neighborhood, our church, our city, and as far away as hard places in the Middle East. We don't have perfect kids who never act impulsively, but we see a growing heart for the people of the world. We are also cultivating passion for the expansion of the Kingdom of Jesus. We pray this will impact their thinking for a lifetime.

So, take a deep breath right here. Some of what you are going through with your teenager, both positively and negatively, is normal because of how the teen brain develops. Gratefully, as parents, we can influence that development by crafting experiences and influencing focus. With God's help we can shape our teenagers to accomplish the unique purpose for which they were created.

Who My Teenager is Not ...

Equally important to comprehending who our teenagers are today is the inverse understanding of who they are not. Even though your teenager has grown tall, filled out, and gotten stronger—bearing the resemblance of an adult—they are not yet mentally or emotionally mature. In other words they still need a guide, they still need boundaries, they still need coaching, maybe now more than ever. Tragically, because it often becomes difficult in ways very different than parenting elementary children, parents of teenagers often either clamp down or let go—not understanding the real needs of their child who is becoming an adult. Teenagers are no longer little children who need instruction for every granular aspect of life. However, they are not yet adults mature in their decision-making abilities, especially under extreme stress. Remember, the characteristic of impulsivity and roller coaster of emotions on any given day can be deceiving. They may look like adults but they need parenting adapted to their teenaged season of life, personality, and demonstrated levels of responsibility. Here are a few clear statements describing who your teenager is not:

- Your teenager is not yet an adult.
- Your teenager is not yet in charge.
- Your teenager is not perfect.
- Your teenager is not immune from making bad decisions.
- Your teenager is not able to process emotions at the same level you are.
- Your teenager is not the parent.

While these statements probably make us seem like the "masters of the obvious," we have learned that these simple concepts are very easy to forget. We often catch ourselves expecting our teenagers to think and process like adults, or we're surprised if they make a bad decision.

Several years ago we moved our children to a new school on the other side of our town. While overall this has turned out to be a great investment and experience, our kids left their friends behind to begin a new life. One of our teenaged daughters quickly made some great friends. She became particularly close with one friend and we were grateful. As parents we are constantly praying about peer relationships and the influence of friends. This seemed to be a great connection, and actually it still is, except for one minor detail. This friend no longer goes to the same school with our daughter.

When our daughter received the news that her friend would be leaving the school, it was especially devastating for her. She would no longer be with her best friend all day every day, though they would still hang out at church and they could still see each other on the weekends when time allowed. This changed the dynamic of our teenager's day-to-day life and she was not happy. Sadness, anger, and a bit of anxiety overwhelmed her. She was processing just like you might expect—unless you were like me and expected her to process it like a forty-year-old man thinks. Angela handled this well understanding who our teenager was in her emotional development as opposed to the "old man maturity" expectations I placed on our girl. Our teen was in need of a listening ear more than a quick solution. I (Angela) remember losing a friend who moved away when I was a pre-teen. I remember the very real pain of loss and the associated grief. Putting myself back in that place of empathy allowed me to understand what my daughter needed. We walked laps and laps for hours in the mall as our teenager conversationally expressed her pain, anger, and fear. At the end of that, I leaned in for a hug and said, "I am going to walk with you through this." That was exactly what our daughter needed. Parenting teens is most effective, as we embrace who they are in their youth and as we understand who they are not.

As sojourners like you, we are learning some things as we go. In light of the content of this chapter we have discovered these five practices in parenting that we find useful:

1. *Learn their unique bent and parent accordingly.*

Understanding that each child is created in the image of God and for a unique purpose helps us, as parents with multiple children, wrap our brains around the fact that each child is so different. Each one has a unique personality, differing natural affinities, individual dreams and passions, and certain skill sets. In light of this it is important that we as parents, especially of teenagers, understand each child's uniqueness and lead them accordingly. In the Bible, the book of Proverbs is a book of wisdom literature and not a promissory note. Proverbs 22:6 says, "Train up a child in the way he should go: even when he is old he will not depart from it."[7] One interpretation of the original language is to train the child according to his or her bent. As parents we work hard to understand that unique bent and train them toward that design for their life. Understanding that affects how we disciple and how we discipline. It gives us insight into what opportunities to afford our teenagers. It helps us coach them into adulthood the way God wants.

2. *Keep the big picture in mind.*

We are learning that it is important to regularly take a step back and look at the big picture. It is easy to get caught in the minutia of the typical day in the life of a parent of teenagers. But step back. Beyond the argument, maybe the disappointment or discouragement, beyond the accolade of the day or the stress of the moment is a grander plan. Take a look at who they are and who they are becoming. When you are tempted to be fearful or frustrated, ask an important question about the real gravity of the situation. "Will this matter in ten years?" Much of what we battle for, demand, or simply become frustrated over as parents of teenagers does not matter ten years from now. Keep it in perspective and remember, relentlessly pursue them and help them chart their course toward all that God designed them to experience for His glory.

3. *Compassion first, wisdom second.*

We are learning that hugs before words make our words able to be heard. Most of the time our teenagers need to know we hear them and we love them. When they know that, they will hear the wisdom we have to share. In our experience, leading with wisdom makes teenagers feel like we are always telling them what to do. A hug first leads them to ask, "What should I do?" Offer compassion laced with patience and follow through with words of wisdom. The way to a teen's head is through his heart. Heart connection is the conduit for wise counsel.

4. *Sleep is important.*

Most studies reveal teenagers need between eight and ten hours of sleep each night. However, many teenagers are sleep deprived. "Research suggests that adolescence brings with it brain-based changes in the regulation of sleep that may contribute to a teen's tendency to stay up late at night. Along with the obvious effects of sleep deprivation, such as fatigue and difficulty maintaining attention, inadequate sleep is a powerful contributor to irritability and depression. Studies of children and adolescents have found that sleep deprivation can increase impulsive behavior; some researchers report finding that it is a factor in delinquency. Adequate sleep is central to physical and emotional health."[8] We are discovering that even as we protected sleep time for our kids when they were infants, it is just as important to encourage a schedule that allows for enough sleep in the teen years. This gives them the best chance at proper brain development and mental health, as well as improving moods and attitudes. Remember when your baby cried when he was tired? He does the same thing as a teenager. The tired cry for a teenager simply manifests itself in different ways. Pursue your teens by making sure they get their sleep. It's good for who they are and who they will be.

5. *What goes in the brain comes out as behavior.*

This is sort of a "no brainer" but it is worth stating. According to the research, what we focus our attention on changes the wiring of our brain. Those wiring changes internally manifest in external behaviors. "As far as the brain is concerned, thought of an action and the action itself have the same effect."[9] Consider the words of Jesus. "You have heard that it was said, 'You shall not commit adultery.' But I say to you that everyone who looks at a woman with lustful intent has already committed adultery with her in his heart."[10] We are relentlessly pursuing our teenagers by teaching them to manage what they put in their brain. This can easily become a point of contention and it is important to strike a proper balance. However, monitored Internet usage, approval of music and movies, and a clear understanding of how our teens use social media, are all part of the pursuit for a pure teenaged heart. Don't grow weary in the pursuit. The how comes later. For now, recall the wise words of David. "How can a young man keep his way pure? By guarding it according to your Word. With my whole heart I seek you; let me not wander from your commandments!"[11] Lift their eyes from their mobile technology and lead them to, "Set your minds on things that are above, not on things that are on earth."[12] Parenting a teenager is a relentless pursuit, but it is crucial. We believe the eternal payoff will be so worth it for our children and the generations that will come from them. Step one is to understand who our teenager is and who he is not.

Endnotes

[1] Genesis 1:27 (ESV)

[2] Psalm 139:13-16 (ESV)

[3] National Institute of Mental Health. (n.d.). *The Teen Brain Still Under Construction.* Retrieved February 25, 2015 from National Institute of Mental Health web site: http://www.nimh.nih.gov/health/publications/the-teen-brain-still-under-construction/index.shtml

[4] Richard Ross, *Accelerate: Parenting Teenagers Toward Adulthood* (Bloomington, IN: CrossBooks, 2013), 10.

[5] William R. Yount, *Created to Learn: A Christian Teacher's Introduction to Educational Psychology* (Nashville, TN: B&H Publishing Group, 2010), 523.

[6] Ibid., 532.

[7] Proverbs 22:6 (ESV)

[8] National Institute of Mental Health. (n.d.). *The Teen Brain Still Under Construction.* Retrieved February 25, 2015 from National Institute of Mental Health web site: http://www.nimh.nih.gov/health/publications/the-teen-brain-still-under-construction/index.shtml

[9] William R. Yount, *Created to Learn: A Christian Teacher's Introduction to Educational Psychology* (Nashville, TN: B&H Publishing Group, 2010), 531.

[10] Matthew 5:27-28 (ESV)

[11] Psalm 119:9-10 (ESV)

[12] Colossians 3:2 (ESV)

Chapter 2

The Importance of Home During Adolescence

Have you ever been overwhelmed, wondering if you are preparing your child to thrive as an adult in an aggressively changing culture? Have you felt anxious about the amount of time left before they graduate? Life speeds up in the years we are parenting teenagers and seemingly becomes more demanding, even overwhelming. There is real pressure. When our children become teenagers it is common for the sound of the clock ticking to "tick-tock, tick-tock" quite loudly in our parental ears. Every birthday comes more quickly. We feel the pressure to teach our kids to be on their own, and to shape them for their future outside of our home. Also with the ticking of the clock comes stress to prepare financially for college or whatever comes next for them. We also are driven to experience life together before the big change when they leave home. On top of that, teenagers have schedules. They work, they play sports, they have to study, they may be involved at church, and they have a social life of their own. They have opportunity like never before to be away on mission trips, school trips, and a host of other activities. If we are not intentional in this season, life can become really chaotic for the family. In this phase it is possible for parents and teenagers to live totally separate lives in which paths rarely cross. The chaotic schedule and the relational chasm due to busyness often breeds contempt in the family—yielding unhealthy teenagers, spiritually, emotionally, and physically. During the teenage years, home is just as important as it has ever been.

Why is home so important?

By God's design, family of origin is the single most important relational experience in a person's lifetime. Even the most secular of psychologists and sociologists would agree that though it is a relatively short period of time that we live at home with the family we are born into, it shapes and impacts all of life. On a practical level, home is where we are shaped for who we will become. The impact of family is baffling in ways. What goes on inside the walls of a home during the formative years of life determines things like who or if we choose to marry, how we will be as a spouse, what kind of parent we are likely to become, how we will live in relationship to God and others, what type of work ethic we'll have, and on and on. It is even more amazing to realize that this experience we are born into called "home" has the tendency to matter for generations either positively or negatively. Home is a natural place of influence and it matters, especially during the teenage years. Intentionality at home is vital!

Home is an issue of worldview. This may seem like a strange statement at first but it is vitally important to understand, especially as we face the challenges of parenting teenagers. If you are like us and are Christians living in the western hemisphere, you live in a land of competing worldviews. The prominent worldview in our culture is called secular humanism. Those who look through this lens to understand the world determine that human reason and philosophical naturalism always trump dogma and faith at the decision making level. Humanism suggests that each person has the individual right and responsibility to determine truth for him or herself. By default, the center of humanism is the individual. This has serious ramifications. For instance, in a family that lives according to a humanistic worldview, teenagers can absolutely do whatever they want and think it does not affect anyone else in the family. For that matter, so can a father or mother. We see evidence of this in western home life each and every day. A consistent lack of submission to parental authority by a teenager is just an expected "teenage" thing in our cultural vernacular. Really, it is rooted in humanism. Fathers and mothers who leave their families in pursuit of personal happiness in the form of another relationship or to chase a dream is not just another common family casualty. These issues are based in worldview. Humanism drives the individual to do what is perceived as best for the individual. This is the norm but this belief system is based in lies. It assumes that the individual is the ultimate source of power, influence, and truth. To many parents who are tired and weary in the moment, this way seems easier. However, this is not the case.

Christians who study the Bible understand the foundational importance of home through the clarifying lens of a biblical worldview. This system of belief contrasts drastically with humanism. The biblical worldview is one of relationship founded in the love of God and the truth of His Word. It also assumes that we affect each other. This is the eastern way of thinking. This view is formed on two elementary truths: we need God and we need each other. According to the Bible, we, as believers are connected. My sin affects you. The way we lead our families affects everyone. The attitudes or actions of a teenager in the home impact each member of the family. The biblical worldview maintains that we do not live in a vacuum but instead live in community.

Perhaps this is best illustrated by comparing and contrasting how an eastern family launches their teenagers into adulthood verses a western family. In general terms in the west we allow almost total independence when choosing next steps for the future. Eighteen is a magic number in our culture. You can vote, fight in a war, and purchase beer in some states. Well-intended parents go into deep debt to finance the dreams of the eighteen-year-old venturing into adulthood. The teenager leaves home to go to college, get a job, or defend our freedom in the military. This young adult eventually dates and marries whomever he deems as his soul mate with little parental involvement. In many cases the teenager grows into an adult who only comes home on holidays. They might live in a different state, start a family, and continue the cycle. The mantra leading into this season of independence that many of us have already heard from our teenagers is, "It's my life!" In the suburbs we ache for community but we live as individuals. We build giant houses on tiny lots and then erect privacy fences so that the neighbors cannot peer into our lives. Sometimes we do not even know the people who live twenty-five feet from our bedroom windows. These are the effects of individualism. Be sure, we are for education, for marriage, for neighborhoods, for teenagers becoming adults who live on mission for Christ in foreign lands for His glory and kingdom. The contrast however with eastern cultures steeped in a relational worldview is stark.

Generally speaking, the cultures of the East embrace the relational worldview of the Bible including the Jewish Torah. Even the Koran[1] touts a relational worldview. It's interesting that whether you are Christian, Jew, or Muslim, in the East your understanding of family is clearly relational and not individualistic. Life there is about "we" not "me." While the East is wrought with difficulty and in some cases atrocity as you likely know, there is more adherence to a relational, biblical worldview in regards to family at the grass roots level. Teenagers in the East are often already working the family business. In many countries in the East, all of the young men join the military. This is part of the experience and drives home the core value of "we" instead of "me." In Israel, the women join the military as well. Education is of high value in the eastern cultures. Often, upon the completion of education, the teenager who has become a young adult comes home to continue in the chosen work of the family. They will likely live with family, as this is an unwritten expectation. Sometimes in the East, marriages are arranged. This seems appalling from a western perspective and it can be difficult but think about the worldview behind that tradition. It is relational. It is possible that parents know their growing children better than those children know themselves. In wisdom, parents in these cultures believe they can choose a spouse for their child better than that young adult son or daughter ever could. Why? They have seen them grow up, they know their bents, and they know their needs. Whether a marriage is arranged or not, often a new section is added to the top or the side of the family home for the newly married couple to live, have children, and start the cycle all over again. Think of it, grandparents are significant in the lives of teenagers. Parents have an older generation from which to draw wisdom when parenting becomes overwhelming. Aunts and uncles are influential in the lives of teenagers. Cousins grow up together and really know each other. This is the concept of family in the East. In the West, our kids want to leave home forever and we encourage it. In the East, people often come home to invest in the family and community.

When the foundational understanding of home is derived from the pages of the Scripture, four reasons emerge, among others, declaring the importance of home by God's design.

1. *Home is important for love and stability.*

Home, in the best case, is a relational experience in our lives—founded in true love while providing stability for all of life. This is especially important during the teenage years. When a child is literally morphing into an adult, love and stability are significant. Their world at school, online, even at church, can be tough to navigate and often borderlines on cruel and unusual. Couple that with raging hormones, body image issues, and the desire to be known and loved for who they are—the need for home as a haven for love and stability is evident. We often say in our family, "The battle is in the world. Family is not a place of attack. It is a place of love and security. You are safe here." Truly we mean it, although home can easily deteriorate into a place of pain if we avoid the difficulty of parenting relentlessly.

What kind of love provides the stability we are talking about? The Bible describes this kind of love in 1 Corinthians 13:4 declares that love is like this: "Love is patient and kind; love does not envy or boast; it is not arrogant or rude. It does not insist on its own way; it is not irritable or resentful; it does not rejoice at wrongdoing, but rejoices with the truth. Love bears all things, believes all things, hope all things, endures all things. Love never ends."[2] It is this kind of love that makes home stable and secure for our teenagers even when they seemingly don't deserve it. This love is compassionate but it is tough. It can be counted on and for a teenager, that kind of love is necessary. This simple Scripture is also a guide for us in the tough times. How do we show love in a parenting situation with one of our teenagers that really makes us want to yell and scream and punch holes in the walls? Or, throw up our hands in desperation and defeat? Sometimes it helps just to remember the love that our Father has shown us as His sometimes-difficult kids.

2. *Home is important for spiritual formation and the shaping of people.*

When God led his people out of Egypt and before they entered the Promised Land, He gave them clear instructions about building a culture and community that would honor Him. It largely depended on the leaders of individual families in partnership with the broader faith community. "Hear, O Israel: The LORD our God, the LORD is one. You shall love the LORD your God with all your heart and with all your soul and with all your might. And these words that I command you today shall be on your heart. You shall teach them diligently to your children, and shall talk of them when you sit in your house, and when you walk by the way, and when you lie down, and when you rise."[3]

This pattern is important for the spiritual formation of our children today. It is a really simple concept. As parents in the context of our homes and in community with other believers, we authentically demonstrate what it means to love God with all of our being. This does not mean that we somehow act in a perfect way; it means that we are authentic. We love God enough to repent when we sin. We demonstrate walking with God consistently over time and our kids observe our life in Christ. We demonstrate growth in Christ. We keep the Word on our hearts and in the center of our homes. Intentionally we talk about the Scriptures and God's way of living in the ordinary, mundane, "every days" of life as we walk along the road, sit at home, go to bed, and wake up. In this way, home is vitally important to the faith formation of our teenagers. Just a side note: As ministry leaders in three different churches, we have seen parents give up on home as a conduit for spiritual growth during the adolescent years. While it may be more difficult than when our children were young, the teen years are some of the most faith-forming years of life. The concept of spiritual formation from Deuteronomy 6 is clear and relatively simple. Practically it takes work and intentionality. For a simple and intentional plan for leading all of your children including your teenagers spiritually, get your hands on a copy of *The Legacy Path: Discover Intentional Spiritual Parenting*. In it, we lay out a path for parents composed of seven milestones allowing you to understand where you are leading your teenagers. We also show you what to do along the way by teaching you three important disciplines to build into your home life including leading a faith talk, capturing God moments as they happen, and celebrating milestones along the way.[4]

LEGACY
MILESTONES

 1 Child/Parent Dedication

2 Salvation & Baptism

3 Preparing for Adolescence

 4 Purity for Life

5 Rite of Passage

6 High School Graduation

7 Life in Christ

3. *Home is important for generational influence and legacy.*

God designed home with more than one generation in mind. When we invest love and faith in our teenagers, we are in fact making an investment in the generations to come, even those generations that we will never meet face to face. Imagine the amount of influence you have on so many people through your parenting relationship with your teenager. Generational legacy is one of the Great Designer's many purposes for the home. In Psalm 78:4-7, the writer depicts the important effects of passing on the promises of God and His faithful character, as evidenced by His deeds, to the next generation. "We will not hide them from their children, but tell to the coming generation the glorious deeds of the LORD, and his might, and the wonders that he has done. He established a testimony in Jacob and appointed a law in Israel, which he commanded our fathers to teach to their children, that the next generation might know them, the children yet unborn, and arise and tell them to their children, so that they should set their hope in God and not forget the works of God, but keep his commandments."[5] Home is important for generational legacy.

Several years ago our family discovered a letter from Jiddo (Arabic for "grandfather"). Jiddo died when I (Angela) was ten years old. He is from the Lebanese side of our family and grew up in a time and place where it cost to be Christian because of the religious difficulties between Islam, Maronite Christians, Orthodoxy, and evangelical (born-again) Christians. As a disciple of Jesus, and an easterner for that matter, Jiddo understood the importance of family and generational legacy. He evidenced this with his sacrifices, his deep commitment to family, a heart for his entire family to know the true Jesus, and his passion for the generations that would flow from the Abboud family. Jiddo wrote a letter in Arabic from Tripoli, Lebanon, in 1971 to his first-born grandson, George, my older brother. Note the content of the letter as translated by my father, Edmond.

My grandson George,

May God bless your future.

I am writing to you even though you have not lived long in this world.

I am writing to you this letter because you are a very special human being to me.

My heart pounds with happiness and joy for your arrival into this world.

I plead for you with the Holy God to protect you and to grant you good health, happiness and success.

My request to God is to make you one that your parents and us and the whole world will be very proud of and that you will be successful in your future and in every thing that you try.

I do not think that this expectation of you is too difficult and a burden on you because you are the son of my beloved son, Edmond, and especially because you have a mother who is exemplary in her gentleness, beauty and education and so do not be surprised at your natural inclinations and qualifications.

Indeed, I might be the first man in this world to think about writing to a baby of your age but to me you are the whole world, all of it!

So I ask you to please respect and uphold your parent's reputation, and that you will be obedient, loving, generous and helpful to others.

The world is fading out but the fruits of good works are lasting forever and will please God. History remembers the works of good people and the fruits of their completeness because God will walk with them and so do not be afraid of any harm if your works are right.

Clearly the heart of the older generation to love God and tell the stories of faithfulness to the Lord impacts the next generations. Our homes and consequently how we lead our teenagers now, mysteriously, influence the faith legacy of the household and likely the culture. Home is important for generational influence and legacy.

4. *Home is important for sanctification.*

Recently we were going through a challenge in parenting. The kind of struggle that leaves you feeling sort of worthless, baffled, and hurt. The kind of hurt that makes you question all that you have or haven't done as a parent. We reached out to an older friend who has been there many times as a parent. It was the right move. His wisdom gave us comfort and hope. Perhaps the most clarifying statement that he made was this: "Family hurts the most because it is the place you love the most." He said, "Home is sanctifying and sometimes that is painful." He is right. Home is important for sanctification and it is no less so during the teen years. In a section of Ephesians chapter 5— describing how we should relate to each other as Christians— marriage and family are considered a sanctifying experience. Wives are directed to submit to their husbands as to the Lord and husbands are admonished to love their wives selflessly and sacrificially as Christ loved the church. In Christian marriages, husbands are to love their wives like Christ loved the church and gave Himself for her toward the end of making her holy. Ephesians 5:26 says that He might "sanctify her" through His love. Though no husband has the power to redeem, it is somehow sanctifying both to the husband and to the wife to love in such a way.

Children (including teenagers) and parents are not left out of this sanctifying relationship called family. Ephesians 6:1-4 says, "Children, obey your parents in the Lord, for this is right. Honor your father and mother (this is the first commandment with a promise), that it may go well with you and that you may live long in the land. Fathers, do not provoke your children to anger, but bring them up in the discipline and instruction of the Lord."[6] The home is designed to sanctify people. It is not natural for children to obey their parents. To submit requires an act of the will because of a fear of God and a desire to obey. This simple process of learning to submit at a young age allows a child to become a man or woman who knows how to submit and obey God out of a love relationship with Him. Home is the place children learn this. During the teen years, conflict often ensues over the issue of obedience. Though it can be difficult, we as parents must insist on continued obedience while giving our teenagers increasing freedom as they show responsibility and integrity within given boundaries. Recently, Dr. Richard Ross, professor of youth ministry, spoke at our church on the issues of heart connection and discipline when it comes to teenagers. He encouraged parents to operate under the Moses principle, reminding us of God's blessings and curses for obedience and disobedience issued to the people in the book of Deuteronomy. "Explain to your teenagers, when they obey there will be blessings. They will have more freedom, more responsibility, more trust enabling them to do and experience more. When they disobey there will be curses. Less freedom and less trust will result in the loss of phones, keys, expendable cash, and opportunities with friends. They choose." Now that is clear parenting advice that is sanctifying and not exasperating.

It is easy to frustrate our teenagers. Ephesians 6:4 is a bit daunting when it comes to parenting teenagers. We are instructed to avoid exasperating our children but instead train them in the discipline and instruction of the Lord. There are so many ways to exasperate. Inconsistency is a big one. Think about it this way. Put yourself in the work place environment. If your boss constantly changes his or her expectations, you find yourself trying to hit a moving target. If the ramifications for hitting or not hitting that moving target are not communicated, then you plummet into an impossible and infuriating black hole. How do you please a boss like that? The same is true in parenting. If we fail to bring our children up in the discipline and instruction of the Lord, then they do not have a clear set of expectations. Or, even if we are bringing them up in the teaching of the Lord, but we often change the expectations or consequences out of our own emotional weariness then we likely cause exasperation. Home is a sanctifying experience but remember, it sanctifies best in the context of relational love and stability. In this way, for a teenager and a parent, it is safe to experience sanctification because encouraging, unconditional love is the conduit and vehicle of choice.

Since home is important in all of these ways and more, we as parents must create a home environment that is conducive for parental influence as well as spiritual, emotional, and physical health for every member of the family. We are learning that a home that is most effective for parenting teenagers involves four relentless commitments on our part.

1. *A commitment to peace at home.*

There is a term among our Israeli friends that seems highly appropriate here. "Shalom Bayit" means, peace at home. It's not unusual to be asked, "How is your shalom bayit?" Creating or instilling an environment of peace at home is crucial for the family with teenagers. As we know, the world can be cruel and the teenage world can be especially difficult. Home needs to be a place of safe, secure, and loving relationships fostered in an environment of peace. While serenity is not necessarily an environment to be manufactured apart from dependence on Christ, there are some things we can do to establish tranquility in our homes. First, creating a sense of order in two key areas often lays a great foundation for peace. Home does not need to look perfect but chaos is lessened when everything has a place and a purpose. Intentionally organizing and simplifying the things in our home makes room for peace. Occasionally, when our system of order is neglected, we have had conflict in the morning before school just trying to find that other blue soccer sock so that we can leave on time. When everything has a place and a purpose, a sense of order drives away many of the potentially crazy moments, which, during the teenage years, can easily turn ugly. Remember this equation: misplaced blue soccer sock + tired and hormonal teenager + hurried and exhausted parents = certain avoidable conflict. It seems simple but we think a system of order is so important. In the same vein, creating order by being intentional with the family schedule is lifesaving. Teenagers have a schedule of their own in many ways but it is still the responsibility of parents to help them plan and find life balance. This is good for the entire family. Truthfully we are learning the hard way on this one. We want our children to take advantages of the opportunities afforded to them but there is a point at which it just becomes too much! With three children—home, school, and church are the baseline commitments. After that we lead our kids to choose one extracurricular activity per season if they are motivated toward "extra" endeavors. When we follow this principle it works well. When we cave, we find ourselves lacking peace because of the overly hurried nature of life. Finding time to rest, play, and relax as a family regularly yields deepened heart connection with your teen and an overall aroma of comfort at home. Evaluate your home life. If it is all work and no play, then peace in your home is likely suffering.

2. *A commitment to conversation that is open and often.*

Perhaps the best way to enjoy peace at home during the teenage years is a commitment to conversation at home. At best this starts in the early years of family life before our children become adolescents. But, it is never too late to engage in real conversation. We are finding clear value in open lines of communication. For us, dialogue is a staple around the family table. We wish we had family dinner at home seven nights a week but we do not. However, sitting down around the table three to five times a week during these adolescent years has proven beneficial. Our family table is loud. Yours doesn't have to be. When everyone arrives home from school, practice, and work and we all sit down to a meal prepared at home it is as if time stops for a moment. There is no rushing around to the next item on the schedule. Instead we are just enjoying good food and each other. We pray, we laugh, we cross-talk and get confused, we argue from time to time, and we talk about everything that bubbles to the surface. We find our teenagers are eager to talk and tell about their life experiences in this setting. We think this "sets the table" almost daily for consistent, open conversation. Of course, this is not the only time we communicate but we all know this is a time for connection, which is important to everyone in the home. The family table is a place for conversation, just like sitting in our living room, or going for a walk, or driving along the way, affords opportunities for communication. So what does this communication that affords peace need to be like? Primarily, good conversation has to be framed in relationship and as you know, relationships take time and effort. When communication flows through a healthy relational conduit, conversation can be open and honest in a safe and secure environment. This is often evidenced by the parental commitment to stop the ever-important task and listen to an adolescent who needs to be heard. Likewise, when the relational connection is broken, communication becomes limited. One measure of success we have always maintained for our family life is the extent to which our children expressed themselves openly with us. Not in a disrespectful way but with a "nothing off limits" mindset. Parents take the lead on this one by addressing difficult subject matter in age appropriate ways early on. Probably the easiest illustration is the issue of sex and all of the branching conversations that stem from the subject. We have always wanted our children to embrace a biblical worldview related to God's design for sex so that they could easily see the difference between God's way and the way of the world. I remember numerous conversations with all of our children at relatively young ages because of questions they asked. One of our children came home in first grade asking about oral sex. Another one asked us in kindergarten or first grade why so-and-so had two mommies. We have always answered those kinds of questions by saying something like, "That is a great question. I am so glad you came to me with that question." We avoid adverse reactions, horrible facial gestures or saying anything like, "We don't talk about things like that." Home is absolutely where we talk about "things like that." We are now enjoying teenagers that talk to us about their hurts, pains, joys, and struggles. It is not always perfect. They tend to go to one or the other of us depending on who they have the best relationship with in the moment. It has been our privilege to listen and equip our children, now teenagers, through thick and thin. We have never been more proud as parents than when our daughters feel safe enough to express their innermost thoughts, whether good or bad, so that we can celebrate what God is doing on the one hand, or help them repent and reconcile on the other. It is worth it to commit to communication that is open and often with your teenager.

3. *A commitment to hospitality.*

In a section of Scripture often labeled as "the marks of a true Christian" the Apostle Paul says, "Contribute to the needs of the saints and seek to show hospitality."[7] At first this may seem misplaced. However, if we are discussing the importance of a Christian home, especially in the context of a teenager's life, we cannot neglect the issue of hospitality and the sin of neglecting hospitality as a Christian value and practice. If you were to study the Old and New Testaments you would discover hospitality as a clear characteristic of God's people throughout the ages. Demonstrating friendliness and involving our teenagers in the process is crucial to the development of their view of life. Throughout the years we have provided food and lodging to many. We often host people from our church and our neighborhood in our home. On occasion we host travelers from the other side of the planet and we make it a point to treat all people with an equal sense of belonging when they are in our home. The message to a guest is you are welcome here, you belong here, and we are here to serve you while you are here. Involving our children and teenagers in this process gives them a sense of what it means to love their neighbor as themselves. It is good for them to give up their bed for someone else. It's good for them to forgo a movie with friends to help the family host new members of our church. We are discovering that as our children have become teenagers they are eager to show hospitality and they have learned how to interact with all kinds of people. We show this same kind of hospitality to their friends and this communicates love to our teenagers. It makes our house a great place to be for our teens and their friends because of the aroma of hospitality.

4. *A commitment to authentic faith.*

Since the home is a central environment for God's strategy for spiritual formation, the lack of authenticity is counterproductive and spiritually destructive to a teenager. What do we mean by authentic? Real, not fake. We are all in need of the gospel of Jesus Christ, parents and teenagers alike. We all need grace from God and each other. Keeping this in mind helps us to be the same people at home as we are in every other environment of life including church. The goal here is not perfection but instead same-ness. This means that we are a transparent people. We are full of integrity. We show love and grace to all. When we sin, we repent privately and publically if necessary thus proving our reliance on Christ for righteousness. This demonstration allows a teenager to observe a Christian faith that is not compartmentalized but all encompassing and compelling. It is impossible to fake such a vulnerable and humble faith, especially with a teenager. Commit to authentic faith in your own life which will help you parent more for the heart and less for behavior.

Some Practical Tips for Home Life

1. *Be available for your teenager.*

An adolescent needs a healthy amount of access to his or her parents. Often, parents lack time for simple availability. When a teenager says "Dad, can I ask you a question?" or "Mom, can I show you something?" the answer from you should be "Yes!" When they need to talk late at night, fight the need to work or sleep and lean in to listen. As much as possible, avoid being too busy to be available for them. At some point, if you are never available, they will look to someone else, likely their peers.

2. *Fight isolationism.*

A teenager in the 21st century can isolate like no other time in history. Fight with love. Have technology boundaries both in time allotment and location in the home. Mobile devices need to be used in open environments. Set a limit to headphone time and other methods used to completely isolate themselves from everyone else at home.

3. *Allow some space.*

At the same time, allow your teenager some alone time. They need time to relax and recharge. Depending on their personality, they may recharge best by themselves. In the heat of disagreement, it is sometimes best to let them go and vent alone before you continue the discussion. Everyone needs some space from time to time.

4. *Be willing to help them with homework.*

Allowing our teenagers to be around us at night in the kitchen or family room while doing their homework is proving to be a way that we can show our teenagers we care about what they are working on. More often than not they ask questions that cause each of us some "work" at a time of evening when we are feeling tired. It is worth the sacrifice to struggle through with our teenagers and to cheer them on in their hard work.

5. *Protect Sunday as a time of Sabbath.*

While it may seem archaic, we are commanded in Scripture to practice Sabbath principles including worship with other believers, time for family, rest, and play. This spiritual rhythm indicates a clear love for God and His way of living and bears the fruit of relationships and health in the family. We are not legalistic about Sunday but we enjoy it together.

6. *Play more.*

Find ways to play with your teenagers. Involve yourself in what they love and do it with them. This may mean shooting baskets in the driveway or throwing a football. In our family this has meant getting a dog and buying some kayaks. Whatever you like to do for fun together, do it now because time is passing quickly.

Home is critically important in the adolescent years.

Endnotes

[1] Though an eastern document reflecting the relational worldview, the Koran does not speak of salvation by grace through faith in Jesus Christ alone and should not be considered the inerrant Word of God.

[2] 1 Corinthians 13:4-8 (ESV)

[3] Deuteronomy 6:4-7 (ESV)

[4] Brian Haynes, *The Legacy Path: Discover Intentional Spiritual Parenting* (Nashville, TN: Randall House, 2011).

[5] Psalm 78:4-7 (ESV)

[6] Ephesians 6:1-4 (ESV)

[7] Romans 12:13 (ESV)

Chapter 3

Tireless Compassion ... Or Driven Insensitivity

How can we exhibit tireless compassion when life is so exhausting? Most parents of teenagers are walking the planet in a general state of hurriedness causing weariness and often a low compassion quotient. Instead of kindheartedness, the relationship with our teenager may be characterized by driven insensitivity. It is a humbling notion to think that God uses parental concern as an illustration we can understand to convey His compassion toward all who fear Him. According to Psalm 103:13, "As a father shows compassion to his children, so the LORD shows compassion to those who fear him." During the teenaged years, parents need to intentionally offer what we will term "tireless compassion."

This feeling of sympathy is a form of love aroused within us when we are confronted with those who suffer or are vulnerable. Tireless compassion is the kind of care that never grows weary. It is the kind of consideration that is certain; the kind that one can rely on. As a parent, offering tireless compassion means no matter how busy you feel or how important your tasks or responsibilities seem in comparison to your teenaged son or daughters' perceivably small or short-term problem, we stop and offer this gift to them. As you likely know, exhibiting compassion like this is not always easy but our children need it desperately.

It can be really difficult to offer tireless compassion when your teenager postures as semi-disrespectful, disobedient, or completely aloof. Since most teenagers have moments in all of these categories, we need to learn to be compassionate even when we feel opposed, used, or unheard. Often disrespect or disconnection is a mask for real pain that a teenager is feeling. This is precisely when we need to offer the most compassion, even though we are tempted to project anger or avoidance. Think about the parable Jesus told of the prodigal son in Luke 15:11-32. The father has two sons. The younger son asks the father to give him his rightful inheritance, now. There is a selfish teenager for you. The father decides to go ahead and divide his property and wealth between the boys. A few days later the younger son packed up and took a journey to a faraway place. There he spent everything his father had given him. Again, the teenaged son exhibits selfishness. He has taken a lifetime of the fathers' earned wealth and squandered it in what Jesus describes as "reckless living." So far, it seems as if the father is just a source of money to finance a very self-centered lifestyle. How does the father feel? Angry? Hurt? Used? Abused? Soon the young man found himself in need, having spent all that he had. He landed a job feeding pigs. He was so hungry that he longed to eat the slop that the pigs ate. In that moment of humility, he thought about home. He thought about his father and realized that his father's servants had more than enough to eat. He decided to go home and beg his father to let him come back, not as a son, but as a servant. He rightly thought he no longer deserved to be called "son." So, he went home. And "while he was still a long way off, his father saw him and felt compassion, and ran and embraced him and kissed him."[1] Though the story continues, let's stop here to focus on the compassion of the father in the first moments that he sees his son. This boy literally took the father's money and ran. In this parable, we do not find a father who is bitter, but one who is broken. He longingly awaits his son's return. When he sees him, it says that he felt compassion. This means the son had been on his father's mind a lot. There is an eagerness on the part of the father to be reunited with his son. He runs to him and demonstrates his compassion with affection. No lecture or stern words, just hugs and kisses. The story continues. As the son becomes lowly like a servant seeking forgiveness, the father calls for the best robe to be put on his back, the families' ring to be put on his finger, and shoes for his feet. A celebration ensues because the son who was lost now is found. In this story, compassion gives way to grace and celebration. The son instantly knows what it means to be loved relentlessly because of the father's compassion. Though it's just a parable, stories like this in modern life go differently all the time. Compassion is a choice even when it is not a feeling.

Several years ago our family made a significant life transition that required leaving our friends and family on the west side of Houston to lead a church and Christian school on the southeast side of the city. Houston is such a large metropolis that the move required geographic and relational disconnect from everything our children had really ever known. My "exciting" call to serve as a pastor on the other side of town was a point of contention, fear, and grief for our family and especially our daughter. This was a bigger deal than I (Brian) imagined it to be. I call myself out here because Angela was telling me this all along the way, but I did not have ears to hear. In my zeal to follow God's call, I minimized my daughter's pain probably because as a child and adolescent I moved every three or four years. I knew she was hurting and did not want to move, but I did not understand the depth of her pain and in complete honesty, I did not try to understand. I thought to myself, "She will get through this. I always did." I lacked compassion in what became one of the most pivotal moments of her life to this point. In hindsight I would describe myself as a well-intended father exhibiting a driven insensitivity in a difficult transition. In this instance, the need my daughter had from her father was a tireless effort of compassion. Instead, she received driven insensitivity. The rest is her story to tell.

What I can tell you is that my lack of compassion caused my daughter to hurt and feel angry towards me so much so that I almost lost my voice with her after years of "walking the path" together. She didn't need a milestone, or a God moment, or a faith talk. She needed a compassionate father who would seek to understand her and console her even if the effort felt constant and draining to me. As a father, in those days, I felt exhausted and overcome by the exceptional demands at work, leaving me little emotional room for compassion. In my life, if there were any instance that I could call a "do over" on, it would be this one.

As parents we have learned the importance of tireless compassion. When our children were younger, they went to school every day wearing a backpack. No matter how much goodness we packed in that backpack as we sent them off to school in the morning, the backpack came home with entirely different contents. Every teacher and coach they encountered during the day filled the backpack with assignments and expectations, adding a level of stress to their young lives that sometimes was not healthy. On top of that, other students often added emotional "content" to the backpacks, weighing our children down. A mean word, rolled eyes, or other discouraging experiences often filled the backpacks by the time they returned home. There were days we could see the discouragement on their faces. Other days we did not see it so plainly, but over time the backpacks got heavier and heavier until one day they could not bear the weight of them. They needed someone to help them unload the bags; physically, emotionally, spiritually, or all the above. We find that compassion is the tool necessary to lighten the load. Compassion is a gift. Have you ever heard anyone say that they were shown too much compassion as a child?

The idea of offering your child kindheartedness may seem elementary and natural to you but for many, it is not. Why would you as a parent work hard to offer tireless compassion? We are experiencing four strong reasons.

1. *Compassion grants us influence and the right to be heard.*

Lack of compassion, especially in moments of need, builds invisible, emotional walls between parents and teenagers that will be instantly felt when your influence is most necessary in the life of your teenager. Things begin to change when a child becomes an adolescent. When our children are young we are able to lead them with our positional authority. Though it is not good or even healthy to lead them only by positional authority, it is possible until they start thinking for themselves. Clearly, children need compassion and heart connection for emotional health and spiritual growth and it would be terrible to mistakenly undermine that truth here. While it is right for our children to obey their parents, by the time they are teenagers, typically, positional authority is not enough to give a parent real influence in the life of a teen. Influence no longer comes just because you are "the mom" or "the dad." Influence is earned in the life of a teenager. One way that influence is earned is through regular deposits of compassion. It is true in your life, too. Think about it. Who are you most likely to bear your soul with or seek advice from? It is likely someone who has a track record of showing you understanding. Your teenager is the same way. If you want influence, offer your child compassion.

2. *Compassion paints a proper picture of God's love for our children.*

Back to Psalm 103:13. "As a father shows compassion to his children, so the LORD shows compassion to those who fear him." Parents who demonstrate tireless compassion help teenagers see a believable picture of their perfect Father's sense of compassion for them. Of course when we lack compassion we skew the picture. In the same episode of driven insensitivity mentioned above, we noticed our daughter verbalizing blame and disdain for God as she processed her pain. We believe part of the reason for her anger with God resulted from the picture of God I (Brian) painted for her with a brush of driven insensitivity.

Thank God, through hours of prayer and a renewed commitment to demonstrated compassion, our daughter now walks in a loving and fruitful relationship with God by His grace. We are glad He is a perfect Father.

3. *Compassion connects hearts.*

We have been in family ministry long enough to observe a pattern in family life during the teenage years. Often we see strained or shallow relationships between parents and teens. Angry feelings among teenagers and their parents are prevalent; breeding contempt. We have heard parents, on so many occasions, heartbreakingly "hating" their teenagers out loud because of relational turmoil and the associated emotional inconvenience. This is so common in fact that the media and music industries often draw clear attention to the issue. Americana suggests that no normal parent and teenager have a good relationship. This cultural representation finds its muse in the all too common heart disconnect phenomena during the teen years. There are many causes for this, some of which we will address in detail in the following chapters. A wise parent cultivating a loving relationship with their teenagers uses authentic and consistent compassion as the glue that connects hearts.

4. *Compassionate parents disciple compassionate teenagers.*

When a child experiences compassion at home, he or she grows into a teenager that understands how to offer compassion in the world. We are not perfect parents at all, but one piece of constant feedback we get about every one of our children is that they are compassionate toward others. It is interesting because they each have completely different personalities. One is a warrior. One is a peacemaker. One is the life of the party. How is it that they all exhibit recognizable compassion? We think it has a lot to do with the demonstration of tireless compassion at home. It might even be shaped by an aversion to driven insensitivity that they have also experienced.

How do we demonstrate compassion? If you are a person who has never received compassion, it can be difficult to understand how to offer it. Compassion is an action beyond a feeling inside of you. For instance, it is possible to feel empathy in your heart for someone without effectively conveying such compassion. So what communicates consideration to our teenagers? Look into their eyes and really listen when they want to be heard. We are listening, not to fix the issue at hand, but to understand the feelings of our teenagers. A common mistake is to try and "fix" the situation. Even with the best of intent, "fixing" language only communicates the desire to alleviate the pain in the most efficient way possible. Teenagers smell a phony a mile away. Usually when we are trying to jump to a quick fix, we just don't have time for the pain. Our compassion quotient is low toward our teenager in moments like that and our driven insensitivity shines through. Typically, our teenagers would rather that we empathize and go through the pain with them as opposed to jumping right to our perceived best solution for them. Have you ever heard these words? "Mom. Dad. Don't cut me off. You're not listening." Maybe you thought to yourself, "Yes I am. And, I just offered to fix your problem." Wise parents realize their teenagers need someone to hear them, sit with them, cry with them, hug them, or even take them for an ice cream and listen some more. In these situations, compassion gives us the opportunity to counsel and coach. Instead of "Mr. or Mrs. Fix it," we become trusted advisors who help our young adult children discover the best solutions to painful or difficult problems no matter how big or small. That is influence earned by exercising tireless compassion.

What keeps loving parents from offering tireless compassion? We identify two common obstacles to compassion that likely resonate with you. First, we are sometimes too busy to offer the levels of compassion our teenagers require. It really does not matter what your role in life is; everyone can have a task list so long that it leaves no room for relationships, especially at home. We are both organized neat freaks in our own quirky ways. When our children were little we had a conversation in the kitchen centered around how hard it is to get things done at home when the kids are constantly asking us to "watch this" or "listen" or to "come play." Somehow God gave us the wisdom to choose the relationship with our children over the accomplishment of tasks. This has proven equally as important in the teen years. All our lives have become busy. Making time for each other is crucial. Adjusting the task list or the schedule to offer compassion is imperative.

Secondly, we are too tired. Recently we attended a graduation ceremony and the speaker began his talk with a discussion on the importance of naps. He said, "When we are infants, we nap all the time. When we become toddlers, we take one or two scheduled naps each day. When we enter the teen years we just tack our naps on to the morning and sleep until noon. By the time we are middle-aged (the season in which many are parenting teenagers), we don't have time for naps. And when we enter our twilight years, we take naps without even meaning to do so." It is all too common in the middle years of life to be so busy that we do not even have time to sleep enough. In fact, not only are we too busy for naps through the day, many of us sleep only five or six hours each night. We become middle-aged zombies trying to help our kids transition from childhood to adulthood. Often, we are just too tired to offer the compassion required. If this is you, maybe you need to adjust your schedule a bit and like us, you may have to learn to offer tireless compassion even when you are worn out. In fact, this is the very reason we titled this chapter "Tireless Compassion." May we speak candidly? Even when we are exhausted, our teenagers still need our compassion. Resist the temptation to avoid the opportunity to listen, empathize, and guide because you are spent. We are learning to cry out to God for strength, energy, and His compassion for our children. When our bodies and minds seem to have nothing left, He is faithful to provide.

One final thought. Christian parenting is compassionate parenting by definition. God is our Father. He exudes compassion. So should we.

Isaiah 49:13 (ESV)

[13] Sing for joy, O heavens, and exult, O earth;
    break forth, O mountains, into singing!
For the Lord has comforted his people
    and will have compassion on his afflicted.

Endnotes

[1] Luke 15:20 (ESV)

Chapter 4

Time ... and Dying to Self

Time is a precious commodity, especially for parents of teenagers. The most effective way we can pursue our teenaged sons and daughters is with our presence, and that requires time. We realize this chapter may be the most practically difficult for many readers because it involves re-prioritizing life, and sometimes that seems impossible. Let us encourage you. The battle for correctly prioritized time is never ending but the payoff is extravagant. Consider a mindset shift regarding time. Instead of thinking about time as resource we spend, think about it as a resource we invest. The analogy is solid. When you spend, it is possible to receive instant gratification but that sense of gratification is often depleted in a matter of moments. When you make an investment, your expectation is for a more significant payday later. You realize that you are investing time now for a better return in the future. Relentless parenting utilizes time as a resource to invest. This is a critical shift in our expectations. As parents we are investing for the long haul with our most valuable resource—time.

How should we spend our time as parents of teenagers? Here are five ways we have discovered are helping to reach our goals.

1. *We invest time intentionally to develop one-to-one heart connections; mother to teenager and father to teenager.*

   Developing a proper heart connection with our teens provides the essential relational conduit for any and all influence we hope to have in their lives. Likely your heart connection development began in your adolescent's infancy and continues to this day. There is a simple test to determine if you have a positive or negative heart connection with your child. Do you have relational influence with them? Here's what we mean. Let's just say you have had at least one of those parenting moments with your teenager that ends with you feeling like you tried to do everything right but ultimately you have failed at parenthood completely. Maybe they said something like, "I hate you." Maybe they simply will not speak to you. When the emotional rollercoaster is over, are you able to influence (not manipulate) them from a point of love, to live the right way or correct the wrong? In short, at the end of the day, will they listen to you? If so, you have a solid heart connection. If not, your heart connection probably needs some work.

   Analyze your relationship with your teenager. Do you have a good relationship? Does it need some work? Are you completely disconnected from them? Where are you on the connection spectrum?

   There are many factors that impact the connections we have with our children. Everything from personality to circumstances can present hurdles in the race for connectedness. Your family of origin experience can actually affect your understanding of this. If you had highly effective connections with your parents, you are likely to build the same with your children. If you had little to no relationship with your parents, you may struggle to build heart connections because you lack modeling and experience. All of this can be overcome, if we are relentless with our time investment and with some supernatural help from God.

   So how can we invest our time to build heart connections with our teenaged sons and daughters? First, we need to spend time with them doing what they love to do. We have a friend named Steve who has an amazing connection with his daughter. There are probably many reasons as to why, but one clearly observable reason is the amount of time he has invested with her throughout the years teaching her to hurl a softball with accuracy. He found what she loves to do and invested time with her doing just that. Imagine all the conversation and life lessons that took place, pitch after pitch. Of course, we have to be observant enough to spend time with our kids doing what they like to do, not necessarily what we like to do. I recently had lunch with a dad struggling to connect with his teenager. Dad is an athlete and a coach at heart. He desperately wants to connect with his teenager who loves music, drama, and video games. Developing heart connection for this father meant learning to do things with his son that he did not necessarily enjoy in order to speak his son's "heart connection" language. Discover what your teenager likes to do and do it with them. This simple investment of your time tells them you love them and want to be with them. Giving your time is the foundation of a heart connection.

During the teenage years it is quite possible to focus so much on what has to be done that we neglect to invest time in fun together. We are constantly looking for both small and extravagant ways to create enjoyable, purposeful, shared experiences with our teenagers. Regularly, this looks like a Sunday night trip to the local frozen yogurt shop together. Sometimes we include family friends. We actually started this when our teenagers were very young. It used to be time for us as a married couple to talk in short phrases in between wiping a face or yelling for one of our children to get out of the water feature. This has turned into a time of meaningful, heart-connecting conversation about almost anything. It is a small thing. We invest a couple of hours if we linger and it costs about fifteen dollars. This is a minor, consistent investment for face time with our teenagers that connects our hearts in deeper ways. We think it is important each week to find a time that is guarded

43

as "together time" designed to enjoy each other. Consistency is the key. Think of it like building heart connection with your teenager, one yogurt at a time. By itself, it is not enough. But thirty such small experiences with your 8th or 11th grader in one twelve-month cycle, turns into a solid investment yielding great heart connection.

We also see the benefit of planning fun time together beyond the yogurt shop to create a heart-connecting memory. These are the kind of experiences that will come up later in life. Imagine yourself in a conversation fifteen years from now with your teenager who will then be around thirty. As you are talking, your son or daughter says, "Mom, do you remember that time when we went to... (such-and-such place)." These are the kinds of memorable experiences we need to occasionally invest time in with our teenagers. Getting away gives us unique occasions with our kids. Changing geography allows us to leave behind the pressure of the daily grind, both for the middle-aged parent and the school-aged teen; pending we can put away the mobile devices for that long. It does not necessarily need to be an expensive endeavor, but it should be extended. This year we found inexpensive ways to have some prolonged one-on-one time away with both of our teens. Madelyn accompanied me to a conference I was speaking at in the Seattle area. Since I was already going to serve on behalf of a ministry, the cost to our family was minimal. Maddie and I spent time at the conference, but in the evenings we enjoyed walking around downtown Seattle. We took the ferry to Bainbridge Island one afternoon. We went for a hike, had dinner on the water, and then rode the ferry back to Seattle. I treasure these moments because Maddie, who is quietly book ended by her two extremely verbal siblings, talked with me the entire time. Our heart connection went to a new level. We will never forget those days or the stories that pour from our experiences together in the drizzle of Seattle.

Later in the year, Angela and Hailey got away for few days. Hailey turned sixteen last summer and we gave her a choice.

We could host a gathering of family and friends to celebrate this significant moment in her life or she could get away with her mom for a few days alone in a far away location. She chose time alone with Angela and we chose the beach in Mexico because of frequent flyer points and a Southwest Airlines Vacation promotional package that when combined, provided affordability for our family. Hailey is an adventurer and has the travel bug so this spoke her heart connection language fluently! The travel experience turned out to be less than great because of untimely weather in the layover cities. However, when they finally arrived, they had an amazing time together. They swam in the beautiful ocean, enjoyed great meals together, and had fun enjoying the local culture and entertainment. All of that was a venue for heart connection. Conversations centered on Hailey's dreams for the future. In a safe and slower environment, our daughter took time to express her own convictions about life, relationships, and her personal integrity. Truly, in the days following Angela and Hailey's arrival back home, their deepened heart connection was noticeable to me. There is something just a little different about their relationship because of the fun shared experience they had together.

Investing time to connect with our teenagers in ways that speak to the heart is always a wise investment of time. We are a conservative family when it comes to our resources, but we see clearly the benefit of investing time and money for heart connection experiences. Angela received an unexpected gift on the way home from Mexico on yet another flight delay. Our sixteen-year-old daughter was sitting next to a middle school student and they began to talk. The "middle-schooler" began to tell our daughter about all the things she was experiencing in junior high and the struggles she was having with peer pressure. Angela was privileged to listen to our daughter discuss finding her identity in Christ with another student. It was not a fancy speech, but it was truth resulting from years of heart connection development. The fruit of your time investment may be more extensive than you imagine.

2. *We invest time for intentional spiritual formation.*

Since our children were young, we have invested time in the area of faith development. We have a plan. We are convinced, it is not a perfect plan, but it is a road map for us to follow as parents seeking to disciple our children. We detail this plan in the book *Legacy Path: Discover Intentional Spiritual Parenting.* We have been walking this path with our now teenagers for years. In our unique positions as leaders in the local church, we have had opportunity to partner with many parents to equip them in leading their children along this path of spiritual formation. One of the common themes we noticed through the years is that many parents seem to become much less intentional about discipling their children as they became teenagers. As parents of teenagers ourselves now, we can understand why. Leading a teenager spiritually is much different than leading an eight-year-old in this way. It is more challenging in that life is busier, sometimes teenagers do not want to hang out with their parents for a faith conversation, and life is more complicated. Hormones are flaring, personalities are clashing, and ideology is being formed by voices outside of church and home. It is in this time that parents need to become relentless about investing time for spiritual formation. By way of review, this works and we are tempted to say only works, in the context of heart connection.

Think about investing time for the spiritual formation of your teenager in these ways. Make time for God moments. These are moments along the way that give us the opportunity to shape our teenagers with a biblical worldview. God moments are prayed for but not planned. This week we were helping our teenager with a psychology paper on gender identity issues for a course she is taking at a local community college. The textbook is secular in nature and approaches the issue of gender identity as such. This led to a beautiful conversation about the differences between the biblical and the secular worldviews. We were even able to discuss how to engage the secular worldview from a biblical perspective in the classroom with a gospel-driven convictional kindness. What an applicable moment. A relentless parent will rearrange life priorities to be present during the teenaged years to take advantage of just such moments.

We also see the importance of time spent reading and discussing the Bible. We call this "faith talk." This has changed a lot for us as our children have become teenagers. We used to spend time every Sunday evening dancing, singing songs, and reading a short Bible story. Now our Faith Talks stem from the Scripture we delve into from our Sunday morning worship experience at church. A lot of times the conversation is casual around a meal utilizing three questions that I (Brian) write for church families to discuss based on the sermon. There are times these conversations are mundane, and other times when they are exhilarating. Certainly this is not the only time we discuss Scriptures during the week, but faith talk is a hub for us. The Bible is clear on God's view for the spiritual formation of the next generation. "And these words that I command you today shall be on your heart. You shall teach them diligently to your children, and shall talk of them when you sit in your house, and when you walk by the way, and when you lie down, and when you rise."[1]

Someone once said that having a teenager helps people become closer to God because they pray a lot more. We are finding much truth to that old adage! There are two forms in which we should invest our time praying with regard to our teenagers. The first form is that of intercession. This is praying "for" our teenagers. While it is tempting for parents of teenagers to place the practice of intentional intercession on the back burner in this season of life (mostly because of busyness), investing time in intercessory prayer for our teenagers has proven results. In fact, intercession is the most powerful influence a parent can have on their child who is racing toward adulthood. To intercede is to go before God, in Jesus' name, on behalf of your child. The reason this is so powerful is that God has the supremacy to affect your teenager's life in ways that are beyond parental abilities. When you intercede, you are going way "over their head" so to speak, calling on their Creator for help, for shaping, for intervention, and for wisdom. We are learning that intercession can be proactive or reactive. Proactively we take the time to intercede for our children daily using the model prayer (Matthew 6:9-13) as our guide. Here is a shortened, generalized, example for clarity:

Our Father in heaven, hallowed be your name. Lord, thank you that you are our perfect Father. Please reveal yourself as a loving Father to (insert your teen's name here). Your name is holy and renown. Would you draw (_____) to revere You and to worship You as holy because of her own desire apart from our desire for her to love You. *Your Kingdom come, Your will be done, on earth as it is in heaven.* Lord, would Your kingdom come in (_____'s) life today. Would Your will be done in (_____'s) life today. Let her be used by You for Your glory in the world. Shape her by Your spirit into a believer who seeks first Your Kingdom. Give her ears to hear Your voice and eyes to see how You are working in the world today. Have Your way with her. *Give us this day our daily bread.* Lord, provide for (_____) in every way—physically, spiritually, and emotionally—today. Help her understand her dependence on You for everything. Help her trust You for the big things and the small things today. *Forgive us our debts as we also have forgiven our debtors.* Lord, convict (_____) of her sins, the ones we know about and the ones we do not. Deal gently with her and give her a tender heart that is sensitive to Your Spirit and quick to repent. Thank You for loving her so much that You sent Your Son to redeem her from her sin. Help (_____) forgive the people that have sinned against her. Heal her wounds and free her from the burden of unforgiveness. *Lead us not into tempta-*

tion but deliver us from evil. Lord, you know the world (_____) walks in today. You know the tricks of the enemy and the ploys of wicked people. Help her not to be led astray by temptation today. Give her the wisdom to see the tricks, lies, and traps. Help her by protecting her from evil that seeks to devour her. Guard her mind and her heart with the truth of Your Word and the power of Your Spirit. Amen.

While this example provides a powerful tool for proactive intercession that will bear fruit, we also must be willing to engage in times of reactive intercession. For us, this usually occurs at crisis points, of which we have experienced our fair share. This kind of prayer involves a cry out to God in a whisper or with a yell. You might find yourself in the fetal position or on your face begging God for help. In moments like these, be quick to pray. Relentless parents engage moments of pain, hurt, or fear with intercession. There is no pattern for this. Just cry out in the ways your heart demands as you intercede for your son or daughter. There will be times, as a parent, that you cannot sleep. There could be many reasons for this but one possibility is God keeping you awake to intercede on behalf of your teenager. You may or may not understand why. Be sensitive and invest the time to intercede.

Devoting time to pray with our teenagers is equally important. We pray with our teenagers in the morning on the way to school and when they go to bed, taking our cue from the Deuteronomy 6 model for spiritual formation. We think they are never too old to connect with before bed. Honestly, we still tuck them in as teenagers a lot like we did when they were little. With three, this takes time because this is one-on-one time. As parents we find ourselves sitting on the edge of the bed in the dark—listening, praying, and blessing. We listen because our teenagers' talk in the dark and every parent of a teenager knows you take real conversation when you can get it. We pray specifically for their felt needs, but every night we pray that they would be people who love God with all of their heart, all of their soul, all of their strength and all of their mind. We pray that they would love people well like Jesus does, all based on Matthew 22:37-40. We also pray blessing over them. We put our hands on their heads and ask the Lord to bless them and keep them and make his face shine on them and be their peace giver based on Aaron's blessing in Numbers 6:24-26.

One final thought about investing time to pray for, and with, our teenagers. Embrace the inconvenient times of prayer. Sometimes when your teenagers are expressing hurt, pain, and concern or when they are celebrating victory we need to take the time right then to minister to them in prayer. While it usually isn't convenient, it always speaks to them. This is true whether we are crying out to God on their behalf to ease their pain or we are praising God with them about a victory in life. It is essential because it communicates two things. First, we depend on God for everything and our prayer demonstrates that. Secondly, when we halt our busy schedules to listen to them and pray we are telling them where they fall on our priority list. What an important investment of time.

3. *We invest time to live our faith in community with other believers.*

We believe it is important to give time each week to worship together as part of a local church. As the church gathers, hopefully teenagers are surrounded by all generations. They join in singing praises and hymns to Jesus with eight-year-olds and eighty-year-olds, understanding that the world is bigger than "teen-world." They hear stories of life change and see evidence of God's handiwork in others. Hopefully, they hear biblical truth preached and gain clarity as they reset for another week in a world full of lies. Sometimes teenagers love church and other times they hate it. It is an ebb and flow dependent on so many changing factors; hormones, mountain top experiences, peer drama, hidden sin, and levels of community to name a few. One of the greatest mistakes Christian parents make is to allow a teenager to disengage from the corporate worship of Jesus Christ each Sunday because he does not feel like it. We have seen this over and over. There is a season in which a teenager is trying to own or disown the faith of his or her parents. We think this is a God-ordained season to form the personal faith of the teenager in preparation for life beyond childhood. Often a teenager will resist going to church. The easy thing for a parent in this moment is to give in to the resistance. We know and have been tempted to cave ourselves. Instead, relentless parents continue to lead, yeah require, their teenager to gather with the family and the church on Sunday morning in honor of Jesus. One or two hours on Sunday is not too much to ask and don't let them sway you into thinking otherwise. They need to experience Christ with the body of Christ more than they can fathom and more than we sometimes realize.

We invest time to be on mission with the church of Jesus Christ together. Believing that Jesus wants all of us to serve others with the gospel according to His words in Matthew 28:18-20, we invest time in mission experience. We do this in our normal circles of influence by practicing our values of relentless love and hands on service to our neighbors, our city, and to people all over the world. This commitment requires an investment of time. We begin when our children are young, serving side-by-side with them in local mission opportunities through our church. By the time they are in middle school we send them on short-term mission experiences as gifted members of the body of Christ. Our strategy is to start near in our region. For example, this past summer our daughter spent a week with our church serving with Galveston Urban Ministry in conjunction with the student ministry of our church. Though she was only 35 minutes from our home, her experiences fueled her passion for Christ, her love for people, and her zeal to serve the poor. Meanwhile, our oldest daughter along with us, served in the Middle East as part of a long-term strategy with the goal of taking the gospel to Islam. Her experiences in working with people very different from her in the name of Jesus, broadened her love for people, her heart for God, and her passion to see others shed the bondage of false religion and experience the freedom of salvation in Christ. We believe time invested on mission accomplishes more to shape our teenagers as disciples of Jesus in a few days than the best teaching in the world could accomplish in a year. If you want your teenagers to become adults who love God and love all kinds of people, invest time together on mission.

4. *We invest time for life coaching.*

During the teen years our role as parents begins to change. In some ways we put on a coaching hat and posture differently in their lives than we have in the past. In this phase we are letting them practice being men and women under the covering of our parenthood. We need to invest time to teach them life skills. It may seem silly or maybe elementary, but it is necessary to say. Teaching our teenagers practical life abilities and letting them practice using those skills before they leave home is critical to their success as young men and women.

So what life skills should we teach them? Start with the skills in which incompetency would wreck a life. In our experience managing money and human relationships are fundamental life skills that become fruitful in proficiency and destructive in incompetency. When our children become teenagers, we give them a nominal allowance and encourage them to work in balanced ways. We are fans of babysitting and mowing yards and opportunities like these that require responsibility yet provide freedom of schedule. We ask our teenagers to take responsibility by paying for certain entertainment options or things they want above and beyond the things that they need. When they have unique opportunities such as mission trips or travel experiences, we ask them to let us partner with them to make it happen. That means they are going to be financially responsible for at least part of the experience. We serve as the bank for their cash. Armed with an excel spreadsheet, we track what they put in and we deduct what they take out to spend. They have access to check what is in their account at any time and they are learning to plan ahead for future expenses or opportunity. All of this is important because our daughters learn that in real life money comes from the work that we do. No work, no money. It sounds like a simple lesson but if more adults had learned this as teenagers … (insert soapbox here.) Teenagers can learn to budget their money so they can accomplish future goals, grand or minute. We also teach them the value of saving and personal generosity toward others and the church. They learn to deal with realities like what it means to not be able to afford something. As time is passing, we are seeing our teenagers make solid decisions about life based on how they are managing their money. We have observed a growing respect and appreciation for the daily supplies we are able to provide as a result of God's provision to us. As we make financial sacrifices for them and for others, we have seen an increase of gratitude from our teens, as well as improved desire to participate in giving to others from their own resources. Ironically, this leads them toward contentment. To neglect teaching them about money before they leave home is like sending them away without knowing how to put their pants on. Maybe worse, because without the life skill to manage money, there will come a day when they won't even be able to buy pants, much less put them on.

A second crucial life skill that parents must invest time to teach is the concept of relationships. Beginning in infancy your children learn how to participate in relationships simply be experiencing your bond with them and by watching your association with others. Our family of origin drastically influences and affects all other relationships in our lifetime. Investing time to love your spouse well, love yourself well, and love your children well, will set the stage for healthy relationships for a lifetime. Beyond this, invest time to talk and repent when you have messed up relationships in front of them. That will be unique to your situation. One night after an unusually stressful day I (Brian) came home feeling like I wanted to punch someone in the face. As I opened the back door and entered our home I saw what I perceived to be three whiney kids treating their mom poorly. I realized later that my initial assessment was not entirely fair or accurate, yet it is what I based my forward actions upon. I began to get angry and snapped at the kids. When Angie tried to correct the situation, I felt disrespected. Conveniently located on the counter was a brand new bag of pretzels. It was filled with air and "crunch" and it beckoned me. I punched the pretzel bag, causing a loud bursting "pop" with pretzels raining down in the kitchen and family room. The impact was negative relationally. I had to invest the time to repent, seek forgiveness, and teach my teenagers that this was no way to treat people even when you feel disrespected. There's a great example of what not to do, basically. Again, this seems simple but to negate a time investment to discuss bad relational behavior leaves a teenager with a model that is unchecked or repentant.

Real discussions about friendship relationships with people of the same sex and the opposite sex are crucial in the teen years. It is such an avoided topic of conversation between parent and teen, maybe because it is uncomfortable or perhaps we simply feel we do not have the time to invest. In our culture, it is critical that we lend clarity to rightness in relationships with others. They have unanswered questions, blanks that need to be filled in, that will either be answered by peers, other influencers, experimentation, or by relentless parents. So, invest talk about existing peer relationships. This means knowing your teenager's friends, asking them questions, and taking time to listen. Keep an open line of communication regarding dating relationships and questions concerning sexuality, and take time to wade in.

Are their other life skills we should teach? Absolutely! Teach them to change a tire, pump gas, wash clothes, clean the house, maintain vehicles, and communicate with people. If you live in governance that allows you to teach your teenager to drive instead of sending them to driving school, then you should teach them. It all requires an investment of one resource—time.

5. *We invest time to serve them.*

While all of parenthood is centered in a servant heart, time invested serving our teenagers helps us pursue them at the heart connection level. In some ways we are serving them daily in simple but key methods. We take time to help them with homework in the evening. On many occasions we tag team editing papers and checking math. We are there for the philosophical questions that flow from literature, psychology, history, and Bible classes. Interestingly enough this small investment speaks to our teenagers so clearly that they return the love by thanking us for helping them. You know teenagers as well as we do. An uncoerced "Thank You" lets you know you have connected at the heart level.

We serve them by volunteering where they are involved. We have coached soccer, led youth ministry small groups, and showed up for a plethora of smaller volunteer opportunities. This is great because volunteerism not only serves them but also gives us relational influence in their world with their teachers, coaches, and peers.

Time at the dinner table is an act of service that speaks volumes. Even with busy schedules, we eat at home together almost every night of the week. This doesn't magically happen. It takes real effort to plan menus, prepare meals, and time everything according to the schedule of the day. The family table brings stability, physical health, and open communication. In one way the old adage is true: The way to a teenager's heart is through his stomach.

At this point you may be asking yourself the question, "Who has time for all of that?" This is precisely the point of the chapter. We are learning that the time investment to pursue the heart of our teenagers requires a death to self, so to speak. In other words, in order to pursue your teenager you are going to have to put some things off that you would like to do in order to prioritize time to invest in him. That is a unique sacrifice in every household dependent upon a number of circumstances that may or may not be under your control. This does not mean that you are trying to make time to be a helicopter parent or to always be in sight of them. That would be a digression toward helping them become an adult. We, as parents of teenagers, are dying to self a bit in order to free up time to invest in the crucial pursuit of our teenager's heart. Time invested now will yield tremendous dividends to the third and fourth generations. Is that worth declining the next job promotion? Is it valuable enough to take a job closer to home so you don't lose three hours a day commuting? Would the sacrifice of living in a smaller house or driving used cars be worth the time you would gain back from the "keeping up with the Jones's" rat race to invest in your son or daughter? The clock is ticking.

The reThink Group has an app called *Legacy Countdown*. We look at it occasionally. You put the birthday of your child in and the app tells you how much time is left before graduation down to the minute. As of today, sixty-eight weeks left for our oldest daughter. It is a sobering reality that drives a willingness to die to self as a parent. The teenage years will not last forever, but how we invest our time as parents during these years are crucial to the adult our teenager is becoming.

Endnotes

[1]Deuteronomy 6:6-7 (ESV)

Chapter 5

Clear Boundaries ...
or Conflict and Chaos

The experience of parenting teenagers is filled with joy and pain. We have experienced some mountaintops and some deep valleys along the way. In particular, there was a season in our journey as parents of teens in which we found ourselves sinking into depression. The despair did not come from a lack of faith in the goodness of God but more from the lack of peace at home. For a few weeks, every time we were together as a family we were fighting or crying. The issue began with a teenager that was angry, hurt, and experiencing the effects of old emotional wounds. Our daughter is verbally expressive and in these terrible moments she said things to us that crushed us. There was not much joy during this season. Rather, our little girl whom we love more than our own lives, expressed hate toward us. We recognized her pain and we knew she did not mean the hurtful words she was using, but it was like a knife through the heart. We sat up one night and talked about all of this. I (Angela) remember saying how much I wish that I could still kiss the hurts away and make it all better. Now, it can't just be fixed. In these trials we must faithfully seek God, pursue our daughter's heart and spirit, and then walk through it with her. We also conversed about the misery we were feeling from the constant agony of the situation. It was in this moment that we as parents put up a boundary to guard our own hearts. We found freedom again in confessing that our joy cannot be based on what we manufacture for our children. That is too much pressure on anyone. The true joy for all of us can only originate from God alone, and it is our job to teach this to our children as we live it out in front of them. This journey is gut-wrenching and impossible on our own. But, we are not alone. It is possible to lead our teenagers by following the path that our holy Father has laid out for us. Along this path is where our steps as parents find assurance, hope, and joy. The boundary became this: Our joy will come from God and not be dependent on our child. This truth changed everything, not only for us but also for our younger children. It proved to be important to let our teenagers know that our lives would go on and that they could not control the "joy factor" of the entire home. This brought health and pushed away dysfunction. Good boundaries protect and bring peace, but the absence of borders yields excessive conflict and chaos.

In their very beneficial book series on boundaries, Dr. Henry Cloud and Dr. John Townsend[1] describe boundaries as property lines that demonstrate the beginning and the end of something. Boundaries are God's design for how life is to be lived best. Limitations apply in every human relationship, including how we manage ourselves. When we are parenting teenagers, establishing and upholding practical boundaries leads to health of the family, health of the teenager, and provides a measure of shalom for parents. Let's face it—during the teen years our children have expanding opportunities in nearly every facet of life. Along with this, levels of freedom typically increase during the teen years and this is good. As parents, we need to expand the borders in a controlled fashion for our children who are becoming adults. This allows a child to become responsible as a man or a woman before leaving home. It is a bit of a dance though. How much freedom do we give them? Where are the lines when it comes to expressing themselves? What are the non-negotiables? Clear boundaries need to be established.

Boundary 1: Honor and Respect

Teenagers, at least in America, have the reputation of being a disrespectful bunch especially when it comes to authority figures. The media they ingest reinforces this identity in our culture. Because the reputation is pervasive in our culture, understanding parents have a tendency to "live with" disrespect because, well, they expect this from teenagers. We are learning that just as we teach our young children important words from the Bible, such as these phrases from Ephesians 6:1-2 , "Children obey your parents" and "Honor your father and mother," we must extend the application of this wisdom into the household filled with teenagers. Our home is not perfect and from time to time there is dishonor and disrespect. We require honor and correct dishonor, every time. This is a really big deal to us. We have both spiritual and pragmatic reasons for this. Spiritually, we are taught in Scripture that blessing comes to the next generation that honors their parents. Also, we know from our own experience as adults, learning to honor our father and mother teaches us to honor God our Father. This is important for your teenager now, and for the adult he will be ten years from now. It plays into how someone honors his future spouse, and how he respects his future children, as well as other people created in the image of God. Honor and respect is a foundational boundary that God puts in place for our best interest. Beyond spiritual reasons, requiring honor and respect of parents and siblings brings a greater sense of peace at home. When teenagers are required to communicate with honor or to follow their parents' leadership with respect, the conflict quotient at home goes down and in effect bolsters trust from parent to teen yielding the blessings of freedom and opportunity. Of course, we have learned through the years, that our children take their cues from how to express honor and respect from us. When we honor each other well, our teenagers have a model for what the expression of honor and respect is like. When our children become teenagers we sense a changing need that they have to also be respected. They often respond well when they are receiving respect as young men and women created in the image of God.

Boundary 2: Trust (Blessings and Curses)

During the teenaged years especially, trust is super important. It is trust that affords parents the ability to slowly let their teenagers become God-honoring adults without breaking the relationship with God or each other. On the other hand, breaking trust is crossing a boundary line and this is followed by consequences. In Deuteronomy chapter 28 God sets up a system for His children entering the Promised Land that He was giving them. After everyone was clear on what the boundaries were according to the Law, God said there would be blessings for obedience and curses for disobedience. This is the same principle we apply when parenting, though we don't actively curse our children. It is our role as parents to make the boundaries clear. As our teenagers exhibit trust, the boundary lines might expand as a result of their obedience. For example, when a teenager becomes a new driver in our house they have a tight boundary circle in which they can drive. They have to let us know where they are going, when they get there, whom they are with, and when they will be home. If they adhere to this boundary, our trust deepens with them and their circle of freedom expands a bit geographically, still with clear boundaries. However, if they infringe on our trust by traveling outside their geographic boundary they are demonstrating disobedience, which is followed by consequences. Examples might be the loss of driving the family vehicle for a period of time, or the cell phone might become ours for a period of time. In other words, broken trust yields less freedom, but proven trust yields opportunity.

Trust is formed over time through small acts of obedience. The expectation is not perfection but instead a heart of obedience. Trust is broken when your teenager lies or manipulates the rules you've set in place. In ministry we have heard just about every example of this. We hear things like kids telling their parents they will be at Bible study but instead meeting a boyfriend or girlfriend for an "out of bounds" encounter. Or, teenagers saying they are going to see an approved movie but actually seeing one that has been prohibited. How about the classic, "I'm spending the night at so-and-so's house; their parents are home …" when really no parents are home. Before you are too hard on your teenagers, have you ever been deceptive? Did you ever break the trust of your parents? Once when I (Brian) was fifteen years old and learning to drive, I "borrowed" my parents' white 1978 Ford LTD and took it for a spin around the neighborhood unbeknownst to them. I did not yet have my license and I certainly did not have permission to take the car. But wouldn't you know, some surrogate grandparents in my neighborhood saw me cruise by their house alone in the great white beast of a vehicle. My parents soon learned of my joy ride. Trust was broken. It's interesting to note that one lie or exhibition of sneakiness has the power to crush the trust levels between a parent and a child even if the teenager has been consistently obedient in the past. What do you do when trust is broken? And as you know, it will be shattered at some point. Again, we take our best cues from how God, our heavenly Father, deals with our lies and deception. Here are some tips.

1. Explore rather than explode. We have learned that explosive outbursts of anger never help the situation. Instead, explore the matter with your child. Ask him what happened even if you think you already know. This is an eyeball-to-eyeball conversation. Let your child tell you what happened, giving them the opportunity to come clean and repent. Their posture and attitude will dictate how the rest of the process plays out.
2. Clarify the boundaries that have been breached. This is an important step because you are reminding the teenager of the boundary that was set previously and agreed upon for their well-being. This assumes that you have had clear conversation with your teenager beforehand.

3. Administer the consequences. There should be loss of freedom or privilege when a teenager lies or manipulates a situation in an effort to grasp more freedom. Think of the ways you have given your teenager advantages based on trust. For us, there are basically three categories: technology, keys, and access to experiences with friends. Simply reduce the level of freedom they have for a season because they broke trust with you or another person in authority over them.
4. Offer grace to the repentant heart. You know your child and you will be able to tell if she is truly contrite or still rebellious. When children are repentant, offer grace. After the consequences have been adhered to, give back the freedom you took away and tell them that you are choosing to trust them again.
5. Tighten boundaries for the unrepentant heart. If your teenager continues to exhibit rebellion, then trust is not mended. When we can't trust our teenagers, then we can't give them freedom. Explain this concept to your children regularly and if their attitude of rebellion continues, operate with tighter boundaries—limiting their freedom as a consequence of their actions. This is tough. It can be as difficult for you as it is for them. It might mean you have to start driving them places again. It will inconvenience you for sure. Be relentless in love. When they finally begin to exhibit repentance, release the shackles, so to speak.

All of this is easier to write than it is to practice. The process of restoring trust with a teenager is not devoid of emotion or argumentation. There are times we have been extremely angry or on the verge of tears. Listen, we have great kids and often thank God for the blessing they are to us and to the world, but it is still hard. We are learning that it is vitally important to go to God in the midst of turmoil—in prayer and intercession for our teenagers and for our own hearts. We seem to have to constantly remind ourselves that we are the parents. On our best days, that saves us from getting sucked into the drama that comes with teenagers and broken trust. On our worst days we have to go for a run, take a walk, or sock a punching bag to have enough levelheadedness to walk through the process in a wise way. But, we do it because that is the essence of being relentless.

Boundary 3: Relationship with Friends (and Boyfriends/Girlfriends)

Relationships are getting tricky in the 21st century for teenagers. Maybe relationships have always been tricky, but we see it clearly as parents of teens. People can appear to be something they are not or vice versa these days in ever increasing ways. Relationships have the potential to be life giving or life taking in so many ways. As parents of teenagers we must teach our children to correctly identify what kinds of relationships are positive for them and which ones might be destructive. Often, our teenagers do not yet have the wisdom they need to understand the difference quickly. So what boundaries should we set up to protect our teenagers who are beginning to wade deeper into the depths of human relationships? For our purposes we will break down teen relationships into two categories: Friends, and friends of the opposite sex.

We all want our teens to have great friends. In fact, so much of who they are and who they are becoming are affected by their peer relationships. This is why we, as parents, have to be relentless when it comes to their friendships. Again, we are not talking about micromanaging our teen's life like a typical helicopter parent. Instead, we are creating healthy relationship boundaries in regards to friends. Wise parents do not dictate friendships, typically, but instead coach teens to choose and maintain friendships inside certain boundaries. Close friendships that are healthy in our teenager's lives are rooted in shared faith. This does not mean that our kids can't have friends of other faith backgrounds or even friends that are atheistic. It does mean, the relationships that are closest, should share a common view of the world through a relationship with Jesus. We have taught this to our kids over time and from an early age. They know people that have access to their heart should have a common worldview. We are not leading them to look for perfect friends but we are asking them to look for friends that share their values because of Christ. This boundary does not guarantee friendships without issues. It simply gives us a common foundation when there are issues. As our kids pursue friendships we gently, and behind the scenes, pursue friendships with their parents. We will plan fun things as entire families to help our teens be secure with the fact that we know the family and are gaining trust. Truly, they have more freedom with their closest friends in Christ than they will have with other friends.

They do have other friends as we mentioned before. We do not think isolating our teens from relationships with people of differing faiths or beliefs teaches them to be the salt and light that Jesus calls them to as His disciples. We want to help them navigate these friendship relationships while they are still living at home and before they head out into the world. These relationships have boundaries. For instance, there have been times that our teenagers have befriended people with very different values. Our boundary is these friendships take place where we have the "home field advantage" so to speak. In our world this will typically involve friendships with cultural Christians (as opposed to disciples of Jesus), Eastern faith backgrounds, or atheists. In any case these friends are invited to our house and our church. There they find love and grace and hopefully are open to the gospel of Jesus. As we see the deepening of our teenager's relationship with Christ and the solidification of their biblical worldview we might make exceptions based on a number of unique factors. We listen intently to our teenagers talk about these friendships and we ask questions. If we sense that our kids are reaping the consequences of being in a friendship with a toxic person, we address it. First we help them identify what's wrong with the relationship. Second, we help them create their own boundary with that friend to ensure they guard their own heart. Finally, we will help them end the relationship in the right way if the need arises. We never leave these relationships unchecked and we never stop teaching our kids how to navigate these waters. This is hard work but worth it.

Early in her teenaged life, one of our daughters had a friendship that turned toxic. We actually knew the parents really well and shared similar values, although not exactly. The drama that poured from this friendship soon became a regular topic of conversation in our home. The discussion often resulted in anger and tears followed by a sense of hurt that was beginning to cause a real wound for our teenager. We continued to listen to and pray about the situation, but we also did the hard work of talking with the parents of our daughter's friend. We worked to reconcile the hurts. At the end of the day we taught our daughter that it was time to create a boundary. This friendship that was once one of the closest, had to be moved into a different category. This involved less time together and proactively choosing not to receive toxic words that this friend often spewed on a bad day. While painful, this was the beginning of teaching our daughter how to deal with relationship conflict in the right way and how to guard her own heart against people whose words we cannot control. Relentless parents lean in here; not to control but to shape and to guard very impressionable hearts.

Most parents we know are secretly, and sometimes not so secretly, mortified by their teenager's relationships with friends of the opposite sex and with good reason. If you listen to public perception and the storyline promoted in secular media, teens live to have sex. In the real world, though hormones are raging, the storyline is a little different than the Hollywood depiction. Did you know God designed you, as a parent to train your teenager how to have relationships with friends of the opposite sex? You are the people God made to help, teach, and lead your child in this regard. We think there are certain boundaries that every parent should set when it comes to dating. First of all, maturity matters. It is a ridiculous thing to observe parents encouraging boyfriend/girlfriend relationships in the younger teen years. While maturity is not necessarily acquired because a person has aged to a certain number of years, our first boundary is that our teenagers cannot date until after they have reached sixteen years of age. We have two very clear reasons for this. Before sixteen they really don't have the developed capacity to live their worldview with integrity in the context of a dating relationship nor should they be put in that situation in our culture. The second reason is that we believe dating, or whatever you choose to call it, is an avenue for marriage. In other words, why light the fire before you can actually do something about it.

We are right in the middle of living this out. Here is our boundary plan. We have to know and approve of anyone our teenager would like to "date." This will involve an invitation to our house to have dinner with the family. This will mean that we need to understand their walk with Christ. We plan to ascertain this simply by asking them to describe their relationship with Jesus. If we are comfortable as parents we will approve of a date with clear boundaries. We need to know where they are going, they need to be back at the time we suggest, and they need to adhere to the plan. You might think this is old fashioned, but before they leave they will understand our view on physical boundaries in the relationship. We will do that in love, but we will do that! Once we have clarified the boundaries, we will offer trust within reason. For us, there is more freedom afforded for group dates like going with a group to a football game or heading to a student ministry event with others. We still need to know when, where, and with whom, but there is accountability in groups beyond ourselves.

Still, dating relationships in the teen years are difficult to navigate. Recently some really good friends stopped by our home for conversation that turned into weeks of counsel and prayer together. Their daughter, with parental approval, began dating a young man that seemed like the perfect "future son-in-law." As the relationship progressed, the parents began to notice very small things that seemed odd. These small episodes turned into controlling moments and emotional manipulation using guilt tactics to demand more time together. For instance, the boyfriend would guilt the girlfriend excessively if she wanted to spend any time with her family or other friends without the boyfriend. At first, this seemed like juvenile relationship difficulties to the parents. Over time, the controlling nature of the boyfriend developed and their daughter became depressed. She cut off relationships with her other friends and the tension between her parents and siblings went through the roof. As the situation worsened and the parents received wise counsel, they began to put up some significant boundaries between the young man and their daughter. The young couple began to communicate, using hidden accounts for texting and messaging. Eventually, the manipulative boyfriend convinced our friend's daughter to move in with him and his parents when she turned eighteen, only a few short months away. Brokenhearted, angry, and in ways lost, these godly Christian parents ended up in our living room weeping and asking, "What do we do now?" They were sure they had done everything just right in this category. Truly, this kind of thing can happen to any parent. In the days ahead, they began to parent relentlessly. They ended the relationship and set communication boundaries. They met with the boy's parents and instilled the serious nature of these boundaries. They lived through "hell" as their daughter detoxed from the relationship and began a counseling process to deal with her side of, "How did this happen?" Today, this family is doing well. Their now adult daughter is healthy in every way and her life is on track for something beautiful. God intervened, the community of faith surrounded her, and her mom and dad parented relentlessly. We think their willingness to do the hard things saved their daughter's life in many ways. This part of life can be difficult, but relentless parenting in the area of dating relationships is crucial.

Boundary 4: Church (Sabbath Principles)

Believe it or not, your teenager will likely go through a season of indifference toward the things of God. It's really not uncommon in our culture although it is painful for Christian parents every time. We have seen parents react to this in many ways. The biggest mistake is for parents to determine that their teen is now old enough to choose their own way with God. While at the end of the day all of our children will walk the path they choose, this way of thinking is very contrary to Scripture. Proverbs 22:6 teaches us to, "Train up a child in the way he should go; even when he is old he will not depart from it." Ephesians 6:4 says, "Fathers, do not provoke your children to anger, but bring them up in the discipline and instruction of the Lord." Just because our teenagers may resist the things of God does not mean that we chunk our biblical role as primary faith trainer in their lives. Instead, we clarify the boundaries. Long ago we committed to lead our family to live what we would call the Sabbath principles of the Bible. In other words, when God commanded us to honor the Sabbath He was requiring one day out of the week for worship and Scriptures with the faith community as well as rest, play, and time with family. This practice has been a true joy in our household. In the seasons where any one of our teenagers is resisting the things of God by saying things like "I don't want to go to church" or "I hate God," and yes, pastors' families experience these seasons, our boundary is a Sabbath boundary. We actually don't make them do everything. We don't make them go to youth group on Wednesday night. We don't make them go on a retreat or whatever other church activity might be afforded them. We do, however, require that they worship with the larger community of faith and at least hear the Scriptures on the Lord's Day. We require them in these moments to attend their small group and we expect them to be with family and rest a bit. "How has this played out?" you ask.

Well, there were some very difficult Sunday mornings to say the least. Sometimes our Sabbath rest felt more like our Sabbath arguments and honestly there were times we felt like caving. However, on the other side of that season, we have a teenager who is pursuing Christ and leading others to Him with authenticity and boldness in this new season. Practice Sabbath in your family and require it of your teen if for no other reason than God gave it to us as one of His ten great boundaries that we might best experience life His way.

Boundary 5: Schedule (Being a Team Player)

The schedule of a teenager has the potential to dictate your life. If you have multiple children, this potential increases exponentially as you likely are aware. As parents, we have to fight for balance in our family life because no one else will. That means boundaries when it comes to schedule. We are in a very busy season of life. Balancing family time, including the schedule of three active children can be extremely difficult. Add to that the constant demands of being a "pastor's family" plus some kingdom ministry outside of our local church and there are not enough hours in the day. Each of our children is in school that creates the demand of homework, projects, and preparation for examinations. Each of our children is involved in church on Sunday and in youth group on Wednesday night. Each of our children is involved in athletics. When school begins in August until it ends in May, we are working to balance life in the midst of all of this. Here are some clear boundaries, some of which we wisely put in place early and others that we learned the hard way.

We begin by prioritizing our schedule. The way we read the Scripture, gathering with our community of faith and our time together as a family is a weekly and first priority. Therefore, we protect Sunday because of the aforementioned Sabbath principles. This actually drives some huge decisions. For instance, all club sports play consistently on Saturdays and Sundays and usually involve travel. Our teenagers have regularly had opportunity to play on club and select athletic teams that promise to catapult their opportunities to play and receive scholarships in college. We have chosen not to play club or select sports because these opportunities invade on worship with our faith family and our family time on Sunday afternoons. Most of our parental peers think we are crazy. We think this is a decision we must make to honor God and to experience a balanced weekly rhythm. We also think this is a great first opportunity for our kids to understand that our biblical worldview affects the priorities of our life together. Don't get me wrong—our kids still play sports and we think this is of significant value. We just choose to play in leagues that don't travel and play the majority of their games on Sunday. When they get to high school, we choose school sports over outside leagues because games are always during the week except for Friday/Saturday tournaments.

A second boundary we adhere to is what we call the 1-1 principle. Each one gets one extracurricular activity per season. This, we learned the hard way in the early teen years. Flattered by opportunity, we allowed one of our daughters to cheer and play soccer in the same season while another was playing volleyball, and another was playing soccer. That three-month season was a train wreck in so many ways. The opportunity was great but the pace just about killed us all. We learned that no matter how great the opportunity appeared, the principle of choosing one extracurricular activity per child per season was crucial for our sanity. In this we ask our teenagers to be team players. You have probably said this very phrase to your teen, "It's not just about you!" We allow each child to choose one or none, when it comes to extra activities, because there are four other people with a life to live in the family. If you cave on this one, you will pay the price!

Boundary 6: Money (Fight Entitlement)

All of the opportunities that present themselves in the lives of a teenager not only require a time investment but they typically cost money. If you allow it, teenagers will urgently drain your bank account in the name of doing really great things or buying something they really need. If there is a constant flow from your bank account to their extracurricular activities or social life, they will tend to become entitled while you become the embodiment of the old adage, "Money doesn't grow on trees!"

Providing your teenager allowance will actually save you money. Require some things around the house and give them allowance for helping. We give our teenagers forty dollars a month. This puts a little spending money in their pockets and teaches them the value of money. When it comes to extra "anything," our answer is typically, "Yes, if you want to pay for it." This would include things like clothes they want but don't really need, a movie they want to go to, or an outing to the local coffee shop with a friend. It is in the deciding whether or not they actually want to spend their money on something "extra" that they learn a valuable lesson. Life costs money and we only have so much of it. Learning this at thirteen squelches entitlement at eighteen.

Boundary 7: Technology (Equip, Monitor, and Empower)

This is such a significant, yet often hidden, arena in which we must parent relentlessly. Our teenagers are natives when it comes to living in a technological land. They have the distinct advantage when it comes to understanding and using the latest and greatest gadgets. The advent of social media as a normalized channel for communication makes teaching our teens to use technology for good and not evil, very important. In the book *Tech Savvy Parenting* by Brian Housman, parents discover some earth shattering statistics related to teens or young adults and how they express themselves sexually through technology. According to Housman:

- 67% of young men and 49% of young women say that viewing porn is an acceptable way to express one's sexuality.

- 64% of college guys and 18% of college women spend time online for Internet sex every week.
- 31% of college guys and 36% of college girls have posted nude/semi-nude images of themselves online.
- 21% of the women and 30% of the men who posted sexual pictures of themselves sent them to someone they wanted to date or hook up with.[2]

This is the result of philosophies and habits formed at home related to the acceptable and healthy use of technology. As parents of teenagers we can create healthy boundaries for our teens that will change the statistics. Especially during the teenage years every account, computer, and personal device should have monitored accountability. As this is installed, it should be accompanied by direct conversation with your teens about the importance of the proper use of technology. We would say, go so far as to use the statistics above to talk about the issues.

It is important to equip and empower your teen in the technological arena. They will use and have access to technology for their entire lives. Using software that blocks access is only productive if there is an assessed problem at home. Software that monitors is more useful because it teaches our teen how to use the web properly, with integrity, while someone else monitors. Each week we receive a report from each account and device. It shows us the amount of time each account or device has been online, what time of the day that usage takes place, and a summarized version of potentially harmful sites that have been visited. We, as parents, also have the software installed on our devices. This shows our teenagers the importance of accountability in the realm of technology throughout life. Relentless parents take time to read the weekly reports and talk with their teens about anything questionable. We believe the privilege of the access to technology must come with the desire to be responsibly accountable. No accountability, no phone, iPad, laptop, etc.

We also set an age boundary. Again, many of our parental peers think we are crazy. We do not allow our teens to have phones until they are entering eighth grade. Even then, we limit the Internet capability of the phone for a season as they are learning to be responsible with their new level of technological freedom. Our reasons are simple. Putting a phone with Internet accessibility into the hands of an older elementary or younger middle-school student is setting them up for failure. It might seem inconvenient but there are two things worth considering. First, everyone around them has a cell phone. So, if they need to tell you they will return to school from their basketball tournament thirty minutes later than the published schedule, they can simply ask a coach, teacher, or friend to use a phone. Second, it is worth a little inconvenience to take the time to equip your teenagers about the acceptable use of technology and then ease them in as they demonstrate maturity.

Boundaries are obviously important as we parent relentlessly. We are not using limitations to create a prison for our teens. Instead we create boundaries for their own emotional, spiritual, and physical health that should lead them on a path to well-deserved privileges and freedoms. When these borders are clear, they help to minimize conflict and chaos in an otherwise crazy season of life.

Endnotes

[1] Henry Cloud and John Townsend, *Boundaries* (Grand Rapids, MI: Zondervan, 1992).
[2] Brian Housman, *Tech Savvy Parenting* (Nashville, TN: Randall House, 2014), 127.

Chapter 6

Words of Power... or Words of Pain

Words are significant. The apostle James describes the power of the tongue when he says: "Look at the ships also: though they are so large and are driven by strong winds, they are guided by a very small rudder wherever the will of the pilot directs. So also the tongue is a small member, yet it boasts of great things" (James 3:4-5). The human tongue is powerful and the words that come from it are life giving or damaging. When it comes to parenting, we believe the power of the tongue is even more influential, because God has given us a special level of influence in the lives of our teenaged children. We have been designed to speak into their lives, so what we say matters more than what everyone else says. This is a power that can edify for the glory of Christ and the health of our child or it can cause the teenage soul to wither from the inside out. Just think about the things your parents have said to you throughout the years. Do you have thoughts of gratitude or tears of pain? Our words matter to our kids.

All words have power, but what should they accomplish? For instance, an authentic compliment from dad to daughter can bolster confidence. The kind and wise words of a mother can lend clarity when life presents a series of options. Over time the consistent "heart" behind our words either encourages and builds up teenagers and in turn deepens our relationship with them, or slowly disconnects us relationally and leaves our level of influence somewhere between minimal and destructive. As we are walking the path of life with our teenagers we have discovered the power of our words for their good and God's glory. We have also made some insane mistakes in this category. We are learning from all of it. As you read this, remember—there is no such thing as a perfect parent.

The best words from a parent to a child are the ones that reflect the heart of Jesus toward His creation no matter the circumstance. Take a step back from your teenager for a moment and think about this. He or she was created in the image of God according to Genesis 1. When God created your teen, He knew everything that would come from her life. He knew our children would be sinners because after all, so are their parents. John 3:16 tells us that God loves the people of the world (including your teenager) so much that He sent his only Son to the world to die and pay the price for the sin of every person who would confess Him as Savior and Lord. God uses words to describe believers like, "child," "son," and "daughter." When we consider our words we have to ask ourselves, "How does God see my teenager?" At the very least He sees them as His creation, designed in His image. He sees them as valuable, loved, and worth sending His Son to rescue them from the penalty of sin. If they authentically confess with their mouth that Jesus is Lord and believe in their heart that God raised Him from the dead, the Scripture declares them saved and God calls them His own. When we keep this in perspective on the great days and in the most frustrating moments, our words are influenced.

Words of Power that Build Up

Edifying words by definition build up your teenager. The best words of edification are authentic and not solely based on performance. A teenager needs his parents to encourage "who he is" more than "what he does." Therefore, words that build up their character, personality, and how God has wired them for His purposes are very important. If encouraging words only come when a teenager hits a homerun, he will think you love him most if he is successful in sports. What happens when he's not playing baseball anymore? When you encourage your child's compassion for others, personal integrity, or sense of humor you are powerfully cultivating what God has put inside them for His purposes. You are edifying "who they are."

When our children were little, Angela began a tradition called, "Ten things I love about you." Some time during the day she would stop each child, look her in the eyes and list ten things she loves about her. I (Brian) am always amazed because it seems like for years she has come up with a different list of ten each time—uniquely created for each child. She would say things such as

- Your smile lights up a room.
- When you think you are alone I hear you singing praises to God at the top of your lungs just for you and Him.
- When I see your dimples I think of my dad and it makes me smile.
- You don't want anyone to be left out.
- When you sense injustice your nature is to fight for justice.
- When you mess up you always say you are sorry and ask for forgiveness.
- You genuinely love people.
- You can't wait to experience new things.
- You are honest.
- When you make a commitment, you keep it.

It was not long before our children began responding with a list of ten things they love about us. In hindsight, this simple exercise provided consistent, proactive edification in their lives. It also taught them how to encourage others.

One Halloween night several years ago we took our kids to the Fall Festival at church. As we walked around, we noticed that our very young daughter was telling everyone something she liked about them. At each game station she would play a game, win some candy of course, and then proceed to tell the volunteer running the game what she liked about them. That night it was as if she had an agenda to bless everyone she met. And truthfully, she did! As our kids have become teenagers we have continued this exercise, seeking to constantly edify them in a crazy world that often tears them down. It's funny; they never run away from hearing ten things we love about them. We are grateful they are learning to love others with their words.

Teenagers need to hear their parents verbalize the simple phrase, "I love you." They need to hear this from us multiple times a day, every day. They need to hear it on the best day of their life and on the worst day of their life. They need to hear it when you are so mad at them that you feel like you could punch a hole in the wall or scream loud enough to shatter glass. They need to hear it often. Dad, for some reason this can be extremely difficult for some of us. *"They know I love them,"* you think to yourself. Verbalize what is true in your heart. It may be that your child does not read your "provision" for their needs as love. Some kids don't believe it until they hear it. We follow the Deuteronomy 6 pattern on this. Though this passage is focused on spiritual formation, its pattern works here. Tell you children you love them when you sit at home, when you walk along the road, when you lie down, and when you get up. For years whenever we are with our children we randomly ask, "Do you want to know a secret?" They always say, "Yes!" Then we always say, "I love you." We know they finally get it when they start saying, "That's not a secret." When our kids leave for school they get a hug, a kiss, and the reminder of "I love you," no matter what. When they go to bed at night we repeat the same thing, no matter what.

We have had some difficult days as parents, especially during the teen years. Please do not hear us dishonoring our children here. We love them all but in their sin and in their very real wounding, especially as teenagers, they can cause pain and discord. There were a series of days in particular that we look back on and view as extremely painful. I say this not because our teenagers committed any of the "top ten sins you never want your kids to commit," but because for a season, there was a real hate for God, His church, and consequently a communicated hate and disrespect for us. These were supercharged days as tensions ran high. They were the kind of days and nights that cause you to ride the emotional rollercoaster from the pinnacles of anger to the depths of despair. Partially, we understood why this was happening. The church can be brutal, especially for pastor's kids. In the beginning of our tenure, a few in our church were especially brutal and our children saw the ugly side of that. In those days one of our teenagers responded with "I hate God and I hate church and because you are the pastor, I hate you." There were explosive moments where we would simply insert, "I love you no matter how brutal you are to me verbally or emotionally. I love you." There were nights we went in our teen's bedrooms to say goodnight when it was obvious we were not welcome. We prayed and said, "I love you no matter what" because it was true. There is nothing any one of our children can say or do to make us stop loving them. In that season of pain, these simple words were words of power. One night our teenager broke down, repented, asked forgiveness and said these words, "No matter what, I love you too." These are words of power. Say, "I love you" often—no matter the circumstance.

Teenagers need to hear parents affirm their unique design and potential. One of the distinct privileges each of us has as parents is to recognize God's unique "bent" in our children especially as it emerges in the teen years. According to the Bible your teenager has been created with a unique personality, gift set, skill set, and passions that set them up to live out God's plan for her life and for His glory in the world. This is what we would call a child's unique "bent." Proverbs 22:6 says, "Train up a child in the way he should go; even when he is old he will not depart from it." In the original language of Scripture this means training up a child according to his unique bent. It is exciting to think that God has a plan and a purpose for our children, and that it's all just beginning to emerge in the teen years. Recognizing their bent, appropriately calling that out, and building on it with our words is almost sacred work. Our words here resonate power and influence. It takes wisdom from God to encourage His plan in your teen's life but it's your privilege under the direction of the Holy Spirit.

There are certain things you will see in your children from an early age—things like compassion, leadership, or servant hood. We start by verbally recognizing these attributes and encouraging them pretty early on. During the teen years we help them find ways to exercise these aspects of their "bent." We have real conversations with our teenagers about the kinds of careers, for lack of a better term, that uniquely suit their bent. Then we encourage them with our words. One of our daughters has a serious concern for justice in her life. We have seen this from a very early age. She communicates well in written and verbal forms. She is a leader. She also has a passion for women and injustices against them. We have encouraged her with words like, "God has placed that sense of justice inside of you for a reason." Or, "God has gifted you with the ability to communicate so that you can get a message out with your life, probably related to justice." Or, "You have a God-given ability to influence people and lead them. Look around; people follow you. God has possibly given you the gift of leadership in order for you to show people where to go and what to do." Recently, on a journey to the Middle East, we saw a passion spark in the heart of our daughter to see justice for refugee women. This was just one more step in living out God's plan in her life for His glory. We followed up on this experience with real words, such as, "One reason God gave you this experience is so you could see His passion for justice and for women living in extreme injustice." Real words. Words of power affirming God's unique plan for her. This year she's applying to colleges. Specifically, she wants to study criminal justice. The rest of the story is yet to be written but right now we are using real words—words of power—to encourage God's plan for her life.

We have another teenaged daughter who is gifted in teaching and singing. Her natural affinity for both has been obvious since she was about three years old. It has been a blessing to encourage her in this by giving her teaching tools like a white board and an "old school" overhead projector for her room so she could teach her youngest sister for fun. We have had the opportunity to encourage her by listening to her practice and sing with determination and gusto at home, church, and school. We are constantly affirming her passion to teach and sing. Our verbal affirmation has given her clarity about how God has designed her. It helps when we use real words with our kids.

Our teenagers need to hear us bless them. They are wired for the blessing of their parents. We can use words to give them just that in small ways and in larger, more significant ways. Words of blessing are words of power. Almost every night we pray blessing over our children. There are dozens and dozens of blessings in the Bible. Perhaps our favorite is Aaron's blessing from Numbers 6:24-26. "The LORD bless you and keep you; the LORD make his face to shine upon you and be gracious to you; the LORD lift up his countenance upon you and give you peace." These kinds of blessings are part of the normal prayer moments we have with our children and for our children. These words of blessing are special because they are words from God that we can read over our children to consecrate them.

Beyond a daily scriptural blessing, we can use words to bless our children in special ways. We use holidays and birthdays to write a personal, parental blessing over our teenagers. Each of our children keep a blessing journal. It is just that—a simple log we bought when they were young to write words of blessing that they can carry with them forever. On their birthdays and at Christmas we write a special blessing and during a specific time on those special days we read the blessing so that everyone who is celebrating with us can hear. These words are especially powerful! They usually bring laughter, blushing, sometimes tears, and always an instilled sense of affirmation from parent to teenager in the presence of the entire family, sometimes including close friends. There is nothing magic in this. It's an exercise of intentionality that requires transparency of heart and the ability to verbalize our emotions and hopes for each child. It is received well because, whether they know it or not, they want our blessing.

A time is coming when your teenagers will leave home. Whether they go to college, join the military, or jump right into life some other way, things will change. Before they go, a special moment could be created to launch them into life with your blessing. We are looking forward to this moment with each of our children, not because they will be leaving home, but because when they leave they will clearly understand they have our blessing. We are not yet sure what the content of the blessing will entail for each of them, but we know it will be unique to God's plan for each one. We know that the words will be powerful because we will convey our love, hopes, and prayers from the depths of our very being. We will read it to them, probably with family and friends present, as we weep tears of grief for the change as well as hope in looking forward to God's plan for them. These will be words of power. Imagine when that eighteen-year-old is forty-five, going through the season of evaluating life, meaning, and purpose. Our bet is, that written parental blessing will not be far off. We imagine it will be read over and over again in the beauty and tragedy of life. In any case, they will know they have our blessing, because they will be able to read it in our own handwriting. This is a passion point for me (Brian) as a pastor who has counseled so many adults wounded and wondering if they ever received their mother or father's blessing. Words of blessing are words of power that continue to edify for a lifetime and just maybe throughout the generations.

Words of Pain that Break Down

There are other words equally as powerful yet terribly destructive when it comes to parenting teenagers. These words break down our children in many ways causing relational disconnection, waning influence, and angry, isolated, even traumatized children. During the teen years the opportunity to use these kinds of words is greater than ever and avoiding them takes a relentless effort on the part of every parent. Here are the words of pain that we, and every parent we know, has stumbled over at one time or another. When these kinds of words emerge as a consistent pattern, we push our teenagers away—the opposite of pursuing their heart.

The use of "You" when disciplining teenagers can become powerfully degrading. The tendency for this is so common in the heat of the moment that we constantly have to remind ourselves not to do this. Here is what it looks like. Your teenager comes in late again. He was supposed to be home by 11:00 PM and it is now 11:15. You hear the car pull up. As the car door closes and footsteps near the door, you begin to fume. You feel disrespected and dishonored. As the door opens and your teen walks in, immediately the apologies begin. After about thirty seconds you interrupt. "I don't want an apology; I want you to be on time. You don't care about the rules we set, and obviously you don't respect us enough to obey. After all we do for you!!! Give me your keys and get in bed!" Have you ever said anything like that?

At first glance this might not seem like a big deal. Herein lies the problem. Think about what our words are saying to our kids. When we say things like "You don't care" and "You don't respect us" we are assaulting their character instead of disciplining the issue. It is actually a shot to the same heart we a working so diligently to pursue. It feels very personal to them and it opens a door for them to believe lies that the enemy (Satan) will whisper in their ears like, "Your parents don't really love you." Truly, your teenager—who is slightly late—probably does care about the rules and does respect you, but he blew it again in regards to the curfew. Discipline is necessary but character assault is not. Take the keys, tell them not to be late again, give them a hug and tell them you are glad they are home safely. Relentless parents avoid character assault by the use of "you" in discipline situations.

Sometimes, we do need to illuminate issues of character. Maybe your teenager is consistently lying. Maybe your son told you he was meeting his friend from football at the movies to watch an approved film when in actuality he met a girl and went to an unapproved film. He just happened to update his social media status at the movies and like that, he's busted. When he walks in the door you begin with, "How was the movie with John?" "Great!" he says. He even tells you about a funny part in the approved movie (that he viewed on the trailer) in order for you to think he really was where he said he would be. Lying is truly a character issue. Your next words are something like, "You are a liar! Give me your phone and keys and then go to bed!" While it is true that he lied and this needs to be addressed swiftly, the leading words in this scenario attack character, destroying the opportunity to shape it. Relentless parents definitely discipline, but in the form of a shaping conversation that ends with consequences resulting in heart change. Be careful with the "You" attacks.

Dogmatic words like "always" and "never" have the potential to cause pain and squelch the pursuit of your teen's heart. More than once we have fallen into this trap. We can remember throwing out phrases like, "You never listen" or "You are always so mean when you don't get your way." While we may have felt like this in the midst of confrontation, these statements were not true. How could they be? To say that our teenager "never" listens is far from the truth. To say that our teenager is "always" mean if things don't go right is a lie. These things have been true in certain instances but they are not even close to fitting in the "always" or "never" categories. Such dogmatic words are personal, verbal assaults that backfire in so many ways. This is the opposite of blessing our teenager. It is almost as if we are cursing them. The heart that we were trying to pursue only builds walls and creates distance to protect itself. Relentless parenting requires wisdom with our words. It is easy to find ourselves frustrated and argumentative with our teenagers. In those moments, be relentless. Walk away if you have to avoid using dogmatic terms that build walls and crush spirits.

There are other words, even more damaging, we would simply call degrading words. These are words used with the clear intent of tearing your teenager down. These words cut deeply, causing wounds that people often live with for a lifetime without the healing counsel of the Holy Spirit. I (Brian) remember a time with one of our teenagers that caused damage because of my destructive words. If there is anything that makes me angry it is when one of our children demonstrates disrespect for their mother. She is so good to them all. She has given her life for them in so many ways. I can't tolerate disrespect of her. In a heated confrontation, as I was deeply offended for my wife, I yelled at one of our teenagers, "That is asinine and dumb!!!! What she heard was, "You are asinine and dumb." Though I didn't mean she was those things, it was close enough for her. She believed I thought she was a jerk. I didn't, but she believed I did. Walls were built that night that took time and the grace of God to tear down. Wounds were caused that took time and grace to heal. In a moment of frustrated expression, I created distance between my teenager and me; the opposite of everything I have ever worked for in her life.

Words of pain like this are far too common even in Christian homes. I have listened often as parents of teenagers confess saying things to their children like, "You are stupid!" "I hate you," or "Life would be so much easier without you." Parents don't generally mean these things, but saying them in fits of anger is as damaging as if you really meant it. Avoid degrading words with your teenagers. They are sure to cause pain and create walls.

Comparing words are also counterproductive. When we compare our teenagers to their siblings, their peers, or even to ourselves, we cause pain. Words like, "Your sister would never do that" or "Why can't you be more like your brother?" Comparison can easily cause resentment, build walls, and kick doors open for the enemy (Satan) to whisper lies into our teenager's thoughts. Lies like, "Your parents love your brother more than they love you. You're second class compared to him." Even comparing our teenagers to ourselves as teens is damaging. After all, there is no comparison. We are different people living in different times in different families of origin. I (Angela) remember clearly being appalled by how one of our teenagers was treating others in our family. It became personal to me as I began receiving the brunt of the emotional expression while managing the conflict. I said, "I would have never said anything like that to anyone in our family." While that's true, the comparison was not fair or helpful. We are wired differently. One of us suppresses our emotions and the other expresses. To compare my teenager to myself as a teenager added insult to injury, not because she didn't want to be like me but because she thought she could not measure up to me. This kind of verbal comparison builds walls and derails the crucial pursuit of our teenager's heart.

I blew it. Now what?

Likely, this chapter has been as humbling for you as it is for us. You may look back and remember times that cause you angst. Maybe you recall something you said to your teenager that you wish you could take back. The Bible actually gives us a process to begin tearing down the walls and restoring relationships. Begin by recognizing your words of pain as sin against your child. When you identify words this way you can deal with them properly. God has never asked us to be perfect parents. Our teenagers don't expect us to be perfect parents. If, however, we are gospel people, then when we sin and the offense is against someone else, we know what to do. Humble yourself. Pray and repent of your sinful words before God Himself. Go to your teenager at a time when you can look him or her in the eyes without distraction. Tell him something like, "When I said you are always mean and that you should be more like your brother, I was wrong. I made an accusation against you that is not true. I sinned against you. I want you to know that I am deeply sorry. I know you are not always mean. I know God didn't create you to be like your brother and I don't want you to be like him. Please forgive me for saying those hurtful words to you." Tell your child that you have repented before God and now you are seeking his forgiveness. Ask for grace.

This kind of repentant, gospel, grace-filled interaction will speak to the heart of your teenager. In this moment of humility and repentance we are actually teaching our kids how to properly restore a relationship with people that we have sinned against. You are also teaching them how they should respond to you when they have sinned against you. This is the first step in tearing down the walls that were created with words of pain and pursuing the heart again with words laced in humility and grace.

Chapter 7

Learn to Listen

It is 5:45 PM. The day has been crazy since we have three kids in three grade levels with three different sets of life stories happening all at the same time. When I walk in the door after a fairly normal day of marriage counseling, construction dialogue, staff meetings, personnel drama, writing, reading, praying, and dealing with the stresses of work and people, all I want to do is go to the bathroom. I really didn't have time. I walk in the door to what seems like a crazy family-owned restaurant. Amazing aroma in the air, along with sounds like clanging cymbals. Committed to making family dinner happen, Angela has been spinning out of control since the first wave of kids arrived home from school. Backpacks and books are everywhere. Angela is giving instructions like, "Fill the glasses with ice" as well as "get the napkins and move your homework from the table." With glasses in one hand and a phone in the other hand, one teenager multi-tasks while watching Hawaii Five-0. She knows that once we sit down for dinner, technology goes off. "The show is almost over, Dad!" The oldest teenager and the youngest are both talking at once as they get napkins. The more they talk over each other, the louder they get. Angela, after a crazy day that I could never survive, is a tornado of goodness—delivering food to the plates. It smells unbelievable! I'm still standing just inside the kitchen watching, holding my bag, sort of frozen and trying to switch gears mentally from the challenges of work to being the husband and dad my family needs. To top it all off, the dog is constantly jumping up and punching me in the gut with his two front paws, over and over again. He's barking "hello" in his best bark. This is what normal looks like just before dinner in our home. When everyone finally sits down and the technology goes off, we pray, and then we listen to each other. We fight for those minutes around the table. Minutes to listen to our teenagers as they eat and download what's on their minds. "Wait, one at a time." "You go first." "OK, what were you saying?" You will have to fight to listen to your teenager but it is worth it. The table is set.

A Teenager Needs to Be Heard

Perhaps, one of the greatest needs of your teenaged child is to be heard. Most teenagers spend the majority of their time "hearing" but not being "heard," especially by their parents. Think about this. Your teenager goes to school and listens to teachers lecture for eight hours a day—for five out of seven days per week. Maybe after school they go to athletic practice or some type of lesson in art or music where they listen to instruction. When they go to church they listen to the preacher, and then they listen to their small group leader. That is a lot of listening. When they are with you they need a chance to process everything they are hearing and experiencing, and this is something you want them to do with you. Teenagers are full of insights and opinions that are often incased in various emotions. Parents who take the time to listen to their teenagers talk demonstrate a true commitment to the relationship and exhibit love in a way that a teenager can understand. Think about yourself for a moment. How do you feel when someone is willing to stop, put down his or her phone, give you eye contact, and actually hear what you have to say? Not just a glance or an "uh-huh" but sincerity in their care for you as they hear your words. That kind of listening is a gift to all of us, communicating love and value. Taking time to listen will make a relational impact for a lifetime. Our teenagers need us to listen to them.

You may be thinking to yourself, "I want to listen but they never talk to me." There are probably many reasons for that, but two are glaring. One is how we teach our teenagers to know if they have been heard or not. Remember, we are their models. They learn everything from us. Often as parents we judge whether or not our teenager is listening to us by whether or not they do what we've asked. In reverse, teenagers learn to judge if we are listening to them by whether or not we do what they asked. You may have experienced this. Your teenager asks for a privilege that you deny and their response is, "Mom, Dad, you are not listening to me." If this is the "scorecard" for being heard, your teenager may quit talking to you because they think you are not listening, because when they speak, you do not do what they ask. This isn't right but it is real. As parents we need to broaden our model for what it means to be heard. Secondly, they may not talk because there may be no margin in our schedule or opportunity in life for them to talk and be heard. Listening to our teens is a must.

Create Opportunities to Listen

In this crazy season of life, no one other than you can create the space needed for quality time to listen to your kids. This is a leadership issue for you as the primary leader in your child's life. Make family dinner happen most nights each week. Fight for it. Dinner together is an opportune sounding board time in your house. Work to create space on Sunday afternoons for being together and listening. Listen at bedtime even when all you want to do is go to bed yourself. Listen in the car when you are headed to the "next thing" in your busy schedule. Make room for time together. Stop tasking, put the phone down, turn off the radio, and prepare to listen. Don't lose those moments together just because your child is now a teenager. On the contrary, pursue them more!

Every teenager is unique, needing different things in order to be heard based on their personalities and modes of expression. Your pursuit of them by listening will be exceptional. For us, our middle child will wait for moments alone to talk. So one of us will help the other two get to bed while the other one stays up for some alone time with her. This is when she talks, so we make it happen in order to listen. This just looks like lounging in the family room together watching a TV show and asking some good questions. She opens right up but the timing has to be right. We realize that we are granted the opportunity to listen to her when we have alone experiences with her. Big things like traveling together or little things like a coffee or ice cream date and walking around the mall do the trick. Anytime we are alone with her we get to listen and this is important clarity for us.

Our oldest teenager is an expressive communicator so it is easier to hear her heart. She will download her day naturally by sharing her thoughts. As she is growing older in her teen years, she is maturing and real conversation is so enjoyable. This semester she has a gap in her Friday morning schedule between her dual credit class at a local junior college and when she is allowed back on campus at her high school. This presents a great opportunity for one of us to meet her for breakfast. This has proven to be a wonderful time of listening to her about her dreams for the future and counseling her on realizing those dreams. It's an opportunity created uniquely to listen to her.

Creating opportunities to listen around significant life moments or growth points that we call milestones is also very effective.[1] A road trip at milestone three for a child who is becoming a teenager is a memorable listening opportunity. Maybe dinner and a walk on the beach for a teenager that is committing to purity for life would work for milestone four. How about a significant experience together at milestone five, rite of passage, for teenagers that are leaving childhood behind to embrace their biblical manhood or womanhood? Each of these growth points affords you the opportunity to create moments to listen.

Of course, you know your teenager better than anyone else. What kind of daily environment do they need in order to be heard? What milestone is coming next that affords you the opportunity to plan some great alone time together in order to listen? Do you still spend time with them as they are going to bed? Maybe you need to reinstate that in order to listen. How about your Sunday? Do you see opportunities to create moments to be together and listen this weekend? What about scheduling a "date" or an "experience" with your teenager—like asking him to accompany you on a business trip or just to go fishing? Whatever your unique plan may be, build in opportunities to listen.

Helpful Strategies for Listening Well

Once we create these occasions to hear our teenagers, we actually need to listen well. This is a difficult exercise for some and natural for others. The following are helpful strategies that we have gleaned not only in listening to our kids but from our marriage and in our work of ministry. Effectively practicing these listening behaviors will help us really understand our children, and will let them know they have been heard.

Our first suggestion is to stop tasking in order to listen. When our children were very young, we noticed that their desire to be heard seemed to always compete with a task that we needed to complete. Whether it was cleaning the kitchen, finishing the yard work before dark, or checking the never-ending e-mails that bombard our phones, there was always something to do other than to listen to our children. This temptation did not change as our children grew older. We had to make a constant decision to stop tasking and listen. We are finding that our teenagers feel pursued when we stop tasking in order to listen to them. When we stop to listen, in that moment, we communicate that nothing in the world is more important than what they have to say. The proof is found in less "Are you listening, Mom or Dad?" inquiries, and receiving more hugs from them instead.

Recently we were talking about our three girls, two of which are teenagers, and an interesting phenomenon that occurs at dinnertime. We thought they would grow out of it but they have not. Each night they fight over who gets to sit by mom. When we asked them why they do this, they agreed that all the other seats are too far away and mom can't hear what they have to say. To us, that said two things. One, mom is a good listener and two, that act of listening is valuable to our daughters who need to be heard. Since dinner is an intentional time for that, the war for the best chair has yet to cease. Any time we stop tasking and truly listen, we connect.

A grand threat to parents effectively listening to their children is our ever-improving technology. Not just because your teenager always has his or her face glued to a device but because we as parents often do as well. For instance, just because you are no longer physically at work, you might have work in your pocket. How many times do you tell you children to wait just a minute while you send an important text or answer a time-sensitive email? Work hard to be present with your teenagers and listen to them when they actually want to talk. There are not many tasks as important as hearing the heart of your teenager.

Did your parents ever tell you as a child, "Look people in the eyes when they are talking to you?" They knew something many of us have forgotten. Making eye contact tells someone that you are listening. I (Angela) learned a big lesson years ago as a manager for an accounts payable department for a corporation. I walked into the position expecting this department to have a cohesive relationship with the purchasing department. What I discovered were years of bad relations bred by layers of miscommunication between the departments. As I sought to understand the problem, it was clear that everyone in both departments felt unheard. The problem was that communication had been limited to phone and email. There was no evidence of effective face-to-face communication. The solution became clear. We needed face time. As we began to actually talk eyeball to eyeball, we developed solutions and problems were solved. I learned that making time to listen the old-fashioned way goes a long way. The same is true in parenting. When we listen to our teenagers we need to make eye contact even if they struggle to do so. Jesus tells us in Matthew 6:22 that the eye is the lamp of the body. Looking into the eyes of your teenager as you listen will tell you if the light is on or off spiritually and emotionally. When they are talking, give them your undivided attention signified by gazing directly into their eyes. In turn they know they are being heard.

When we were going through our own pre-marriage counseling we discovered a listening technique called "reflective listening." Not only has this been an important strategy in our marriage the last twenty years, but also we are finding that it is very effective with our teenagers. Reflective listening requires the listener to return what he believes he is hearing. For instance, if your teenager tells you a long story about how they feel like a coach or a teacher is being unfair to them at school you might respond like this: "So, what I think you are saying is that you feel like you are being treated in an unfair manner by Coach." This simple act of reflecting communicates that you hear and understand the moral of the story that your teenager is telling you. If you know you are going to respond with a reflective statement, you are forced to keep your head in the game while they are talking. Perhaps the greatest advantage to reflective listening is that the technique clarifies what is being communicated. When we reflect, we are making sure we understand what our teenager is really saying, not what we think they are saying as we have heard it through our filter of experiences or a need to quickly provide a solution to a problem. This is a good listening skill for parents to practice with children of any age.

As you reflect on what has been said, demonstrate compassion and understanding. Use words like, "I hear you and I understand." "I'm so sorry." or "You have every right to feel that way." Our teenagers live in a world that normally does not offer them compassion. When we show them consideration we speak to their hearts. Kindness comes naturally for some and for others it is an effort not unlike "listening." In either case, demonstrate compassion that validates and affirms the emotions they are really feeling whether it be jubilation or depression. One of our daughters came to Angela and expressed a struggle and hurt in her life. Her honesty was beautiful but mom's reaction could have been pain, anger, or even disappointment. Instead her response was, "I love you" followed by a long embrace while tears of repentance were shed. Later, in a letter to Angela, our daughter expressed that this response spoke more to her than a lecture ever could have. Most of the time what our teenagers need is a source of compassion and understanding, not a solutions provider. This is especially true when they are bearing their soul.

Resist the urge to quickly fix whatever problem your teenager is communicating to you. Chances are your son or daughter doesn't really want you to fix it. Really, they just want you to understand. In well-intended ways, we often try to fix things because we don't want our children to experience pain or struggle. Yet, this is part of life. Have you ever said things to your teenager like, "Just blow it off" or "Give it a little time; it will get better"? Statements like these are what we call "fix it" statements. They communicate the parental need to quickly pull our teenagers out of an emotional quagmire or the desire to end a conversation so we can get on to whatever is competing for our attention at the moment. They can be well intended but "Mr. or Mrs. Fix It" is not who your teen wants to talk with. They need Dad or Mom who will listen. When our children were little and they would tell me (Brian) about a conflict they were having with someone at school, I would generally say something like, "Do you want me to squash him like a bug tomorrow?" They would laugh and say, "No, Dad." When they became teenagers, I started saying stuff like, "Do you want me to punch his dad in the face tomorrow?" One night one of our girls said, "No Dad, I don't want you to squash him like a bug or punch his dad in the face, I just want you to listen." That was enough for me. Lesson learned.

A subtle yet important aspect of listening involves our non-verbal facial expressions. Parents, we need to control our faces. It sounds insane but it is a real issue. For instance, if your teenager is sharing something and you realize they have made a very stupid choice, you may filter your desire to say, "That is so stupid" while your face is still screaming, "You are so stupid!" Sometimes they hear the non-verbal facial expressions with extreme clarity and with more volume than our words. How about your facial expression when they ask you a question like, "What does copulation mean?" or "Why do people like to have oral sex?" or "What's the big deal about masturbation?" Do you compose yourself enough to get words of wisdom out while your face is screaming, "Why are you asking me this?" If so, it might be the last time your curious son or daughter asks you a question from the "sex" category. Next time they might ask a friend. Our non-verbal communication matters when talking with our kids. Practice self-control over your facial expressions when you are listening to your teenager.

Facilitating Conversations

Sometimes facilitating conversations with teenagers can be difficult. Maybe they don't feel like talking. Or, maybe they are generally introverted or they cannot get a word in over the volume of the other family members. You might find that when you create moments to listen, that it is difficult for them to talk, especially if this is a new experience in your parent-teenager relationship. How can we spur on the conversation in authentic ways so that we can listen?

Begin by asking the right questions. Dinner table or bed-time questions like, "What was the best thing about your day today and what was the worst?" "What are you excited about or what scares you the most?" Use topics that they are involved in to spark conversation. "How did you feel like you played in the soccer game?" "Who did you sit with at lunch today?" "What is your most difficult class at school?" What are your biggest questions about the faith that no one seems to answer well for you?" "Who is your best friend and why?" "What do you hate?" "What or who do you love?" Ask them what they think about current events or popular cultural issues and be willing to listen even if you don't agree. Asking the right questions can open a world of conversation with your teenager.

Of course, asking the right questions in the right way is equally as important. If your questions come across as a bombardment or as an inquisition, likely your teenager will shut down. Ask questions to explore with them and give them room to "whiteboard process." Whiteboard discussions in any environment are beneficial because they are safe. When you get finished with the discussion you simply erase the whiteboard, no harm no foul. We are not asking you to pull out a white board with your teenager, but it is beneficial to have conversations that are safe, which can just be erased at the end.

A few of the greatest questions we have learned to ask our children are simple but meaningful. "What do you need prayer about?" and "Who in your life can we be praying for along with you?" For us, these questions generate great conversations and involve us in the parts of our teenager's world that we don't walk in every day. In fairness, we started asking these questions daily when our children were really little. We think as they have become teens this opportunity for them to be transparent and heard is easy for them because it has always been a safe place with Mom and Dad. It is not always a profound experience. Sometimes we get, "Pray for my math test or my history quiz." So, we do. Sometimes we get, "Nothing right now," and that's OK. Other times we find a hurting heart that needs to weep and be prayed over. Occasionally we find concern expressed for a friend who is in a terrible situation and needs help. We beg God to intervene. Sometimes we hear of situations our teenagers are in with a teacher or coach that they do not know how to properly handle and so we pray with them for wisdom. Often we discover answered prayers and things that need to be celebrated through thanksgiving to God. We think the parental discipline of asking these questions every day yields fruitful opportunities to listen.

The older our teenagers get, the more important it is for us to help them sift their hopes and dreams. Part of training a child up in the way he should go is recognizing how God has wired him uniquely. During the latter teen years, we listen to lead our child toward his place of influence in the world for the glory of Christ. You may observe hints of an emerging destiny in natural gifts and talents displayed over time or in growing areas of interests. A wise parent listens to her teenager in order to hear the dreams God has placed inside him. This is much different than imposing our dreams for our children upon them. This is listening with intentionality in order to graciously draw out the dreams God has put in their hearts for the future. In a way, we are sifting dozens, maybe hundreds of conversations to help them narrow their focus on God's plan for their future. Sometimes this begins by asking the right questions. We are finding that these important opportunities to listen bubble up spontaneously more often than not. It is the best thing when the teenager initiates these conversations. Most of the time if we ask a, "What do you want to do with the rest of your life?" question, we get the answer, "I don't know." However, when one of our kids asks a question like, "Dad, what does Mr. Schroeder do all day every day?" we know that they are expressing interest in the kind of influence in the world that Mr. Schroeder demonstrates. Over time we learn about the passions and interests of our teen by simply listening.

As mentioned earlier in this book, one of our daughters has been expressing interest in multiple specialty areas of the criminal justice field. (Don't hold her or us to this. We are walking through this right now and anything could happen.) This makes sense to us because from her early childhood she has been a kid that is passionate about justice in groups. In her teen years she has become known for her sense of justice among her peers. As we began to see that trait inside her we gave her opportunities through our church to serve among people experiencing extreme levels of injustice. It seems this has only fueled the fire. A few weeks ago she asked us if she could tour the crime lab at our city's police headquarters. We arranged that experience so that she could see an area of secular justice that she is keenly interested in exploring. Now, she is interested in evaluating universities with criminal justice programs. It appears that her God-given bent is slowly narrowing into a place of influence in the world for the glory of Christ. Our understanding along the way has come from observing her strengths, passions, personality, as well as listening to her heart. Who knows exactly what the Lord has for her but we see "listening" as a great tool for shepherding teenagers, like our daughter, toward living their God-given hopes and dreams. A relentless parent gently guides their teen to identify her hopes and dreams. We understand these hopes and dreams practically by listening.

Resist the Need to Always Be Right

I (Brian) made a perpetual mistake in parenting for several years that has been a hard habit to break. In every conversation I had a need to be right. In practice this involved me listening to about half of someone's thought and then inserting my best solution or correct opinion. If there were disagreement or push back against that solution or opinion, I felt disrespected and this pattern impeded my ability to listen to my own children. Often what they were trying to say and what I was hearing (because I only listened to half of what the speaker intended for me to hear) were drastically different. This caused difficult misunderstandings and assumptions. When I became aware of this tendency, it became clear that it was not only in parenting that I lacked listening skills but in other relationships as well. As we as a couple have shared this struggle openly with other parents, we find that a lot of people also battle with the same issue. This happens for a few reasons, such as pride or position. I'm Dad. I must be right. For me, sometimes it had to do with a lack of emotional energy. I wanted to solve the problem and move on. Not effective! As a sojourner who struggles with this, let me encourage you to resist the need to always be right or to instantly provide a solution. Take the time to listen to all of what your teenager needs to say. Ask clarifying questions to make sure you understand what has been conveyed. Take the time to ponder the discussion and consult with your spouse or with another trusted person of wisdom. Interrupting and "shooting from the hip" only causes confusion and someone always gets hurt. Provide wise counsel. Be a relentless parent—not from a need to be correct, stemming from pride, but from a desire to understand your teen and lead him in the way he should go. Learn to listen and you will have your teen's heart.

Endnotes

[1] For more information on milestones read, *The Legacy Path: Discover Intentional Spiritual Parenting* by Brian Haynes or visit www.legacymilestones.com.

Chapter 8

Build Their Identity

Identity has always been an issue when it comes to adolescents. "Who am I?" and "Who am I supposed to be?" are common questions as we navigate youth. Today, identity issues are complex. The media and the culture have stretched the American mantra of "You can be anything you want to be," so far as to include self-determination of personal gender identity and preferences despite physiological design. More than ever before identity is an issue requiring guidance. Parents play a key part in establishing identity in the life of their child. During the teen years this role changes a bit but relentless parents understand it is no less intentional.

The Quest for Identity

The adolescent years will challenge your child's identity to the very core of his being. The question he may not verbalize but will continually ask through this process is "Who am I?" Certain influences in his life are forcing him to ask the question repeatedly. His hormones are changing and surging as he matures, causing rushes of emotions, feelings, and physical responses. Learning to exert self-control when dealing with these hormonally induced feelings is difficult in the teen years and constantly drives kids to ask, "Who am I becoming?" Peers also have an influence on this answer of "Who am I?" Human psychology reveals that the environment we experience every day has a powerful effect on who we are. The teenagers that our children call friends intentionally or unintentionally will have something to say in the quest for identity. The education process also works to fill in the blanks for the teen seeking to understand identity. Depending on the philosophy behind what a student is being taught every day in classes such as science, psychology, literature, history, or sociology—teenagers will learn egregious lies or important truths about the human race. In short, a humanistic philosophy will teach them that their physical identity evolved from the apes, and who they choose to be is up to them entirely. A biblical worldview on the other hand will teach them that God has created them for a reason and a purpose, and that they must seek Him to discover His purpose for their lives. These worldviews are radically opposed to one another! How a teenager is educated will in part shape their identity. Other powerful influences include media in every form. Church is a powerful influence for teenagers who find answers to their quest for identity by studying the Scriptures with others in a community of faith. Finally, and most importantly, parents influence identity with potentially more power than all the other common influences in teen life. Many parents feel helpless, thinking all the other influences in their child's life somehow trumps their own. We understand. The influences of the current culture serve as formidable obstacles for parents to encourage their teens to embrace their identity in Christ. Here is the good news. It is a myth that parental influence has changed in a child's life in the 21st century. In a recent sociological study from Oxford University focused on how faith is passed across generations, the researchers conclude something profound that every parent needs to understand as it relates to shaping the identity of our teenagers. "In short, our results indicate that the decline in parental influence assumed by many has not occurred in the religious beliefs and practices. Rather than rebelling against or abandoning their parents' values and beliefs, a majority of younger generation members today appear to have retained those values and beliefs—while also adapting them into a new historical context."[1] Parents, by God's design, have the upper hand when it comes to influence, even in the 21st century. With that much influence, particularly through the conduit of heart connection, parents have the ability to build identity in the lives of their teenagers. Here's the challenge. As they are asking the questions "Who am I?" and "Who am I supposed to be?" in their search for identity, then relentless parents should constantly reform the questions to "Whose am I?" and "What has He designed me to become?"

Identity in Christ

Our teen's entire life is built on his or her identity, perceived or otherwise. Building truth into her life and reinforcing her true identity in Christ can create a solid worldview by which to base the decisions that will form the rest of her life, eternally. What are the key components, biblically, of a properly formed identity in Christ?

Identity begins with creation. Genesis 1:26-28 are critically forming verses in order for a teenager to understand his true identity. "Then God said, 'Let us make man in our image, after our likeness. And let them have dominion over the fish of the sea and over the birds of the heavens and over the livestock and over all the earth and over every creeping thing that creeps on the earth.' So God created man in his own image, in the image of God he created him; male and female he created them. And God blessed them. And God said to them, 'Be fruitful and multiply and fill the earth and subdue it and have dominion over the fish of the sea and over the birds of the heavens and over every living thing that moves on the earth.' "[2] Understanding the origin, order, and intent of their creation leads a teenager, or any person for that matter, to a sense of personal identity. To accept these verses from Genesis as true, a person learns several things about his own identity. First, God creates people on purpose. A life is no accident but instead fully intentional. Second, people are created in the image of God—meaning that we are different than every other creature, making us special to God. Next we are created male and female. Therefore, from the beginning, God has chosen a physiological and biological identity for us based on the number of chromosomes in our design resulting in anatomy we did not choose. We also learn that God intends for humanity to exercise stewardship and dominion over all other living creatures on the earth. Finally, we discover that it is God's intent for us to be fruitful and multiply from the first man and woman, Adam and Eve, until now. Logically, we deduce that we are all related to Adam and Eve, called to stewardship and multiplication, and that we carry their traits including the propensity to sin. All of this shapes my identity. When we lead our teens to recognize or remember that we are created by God, in His image, for a purpose, we help them see that they are part of something bigger, greater, and that their life is connected to God and to people past, present, and future. This is important for every person. Questions of purpose, connection, and personal identity, even in the most obvious ways such as gender, deserve answers. Relentless parents go back to the beginning and demonstrate the exciting truth that God has created people intentionally and for a purpose. We like to tell our kids, that we all, in Christ, are His kids. Understanding this simplistic yet profound concept will influence a teenager's decisions about life, relationships, sexuality, and so on.

As we are establishing their identity in the creation narrative, we need to build in a clear understanding of the gospel as a grace-filled identity-altering message from God. The gospel is rooted in God's love for His creation and is essential for a personal identity in Christ. Often, even in religious homes, teenagers do not understand the essence of the gospel and how it changes everything, including our identity. We have a problem. Our identity as people created in the image of God is marred. In Genesis chapter three for the first time, people blatantly disobey God. This act of disobedience is commonly referred to as the Fall of Mankind, resulting in sin. As Adam and Eve sinned, so also every person born from their line (that's all of us) was born into sin. This is why our children instinctively know how to disobey, lie, talk back, steal, and cheat. It also explains why you and I continue to struggle against our own pride and flesh even as adults. We were born sinners. This probably won't be hard to prove to your teenager. He might not want to hear it but his life will prove it. Be transparent and also admit that your life proves it as well. Our teenagers already know that. Admitting it makes you real, humble, and in need of the gospel, just like they are in need.

Sin is a problem. Without a remedy, sin defines our identity. Here's what we mean. Ephesians 2:1-3 says, "And you were dead in the trespasses and sins in which you once walked, following the course of this world, following the prince of the power of the air, the spirit that is now at work in the sons of disobedience—among whom we all once lived in the passions of our flesh, carrying out the desires of the body and mind, and were by nature children of wrath, like the rest of mankind."[3] As sinners we are identified in the Scripture as "children of wrath." Scary! In other places the Bible identifies sinners as "enemies" of God.[4] This biblical clarity is important because when we understand the gospel, and when our teenagers receive the gospel, our identity changes. We get a new identity. Jesus called it being "born again." We get a "new life" according to the Scriptures. If your child is a believer, then his identity is formed only in Christ. He is made new. Let's pick up again at Ephesians 2:4-7 where we read, "But God, being rich in mercy, because of the great love with which he loved us, even when we were dead in our trespasses, made us alive together with Christ—by grace you have been saved—and raised us up with him and seated us with him in the heavenly places in Christ Jesus."[5] So, because God is merciful, in Christ, He has changed our status. We have gone from being dead to alive with Christ. We have been given a future with Him in eternity in the heavenly places. Instead of being His enemy because of our sin, we are now reconciled to God by the death of His Son and we are saved by His blood and given a future through His victorious resurrection. An authentic confession of Christ as Lord, and a true belief that He suffered on the cross to death for our sins and then was raised to life means we are saved from the penalty of sin and the wrath of God. It also means that we are changed. Even though we came into sin by Adam, we are made righteous through the man Jesus Christ. In this, our identity completely changes as we leave rebellion behind and by grace receive the righteousness of Christ by His blood. That's really good news!

Sometimes it is hard for us to get our minds around God's demonstration of His love for us. 1 John 4:10 succinctly describes this identity changing love. "In this is love, not that we have loved God but that he loved us and sent his Son to be the propitiation for our sins."[6] "Propitiation" is the appropriate word. It means Jesus bore the penalty of our sin (death) and at the same time endured the righteous wrath of God (crucifixion) as if He were an enemy, so that all of us (who really are enemies of God) might confess Him as Lord, be saved and receive a new identity. That is not religion. That is the gospel and it changes everything about our identity.

Nurturing Your Teen's Identity in Christ

All that being said, cultivating your child's identity in Christ takes wisdom and a relentless effort when she is a teenager. It is really easy to be too "hands off" in this category. It is also a mistake to be too "hands on." There is a balance. Each one of our children is created uniquely by God to glorify Him forever. They have unique passions and, because of their identity in Christ, important spiritual gifts that God has chosen for them. Relentless parenting involves helping them identify and exercise these gifts as they become a person of influence on their way to adulthood. If our teenagers are disciples of Jesus, then the words of our Master apply to them. Jesus said, "You are the light of the world. A city set on a hill cannot be hidden. Nor do people light a lamp and put it under a basket, but on a stand, and it gives light to all in the house. In the same way, let your light shine before others, so that they may see your good works and give glory to your Father who is in heaven."[7] In this sense, every disciple of Jesus is a gospel light to the people of the world for very important and eternal kingdom purposes. Every disciple of Jesus, because of Jesus, is a person of influence, including our teenagers. As parents we want to nurture their uniqueness in their identity in Christ so that they can become the most effective light, or person of influence in the world, for the glory of Christ and the love of people. Our role is to help them find their place in the world as a disciple of Jesus for the Kingdom's sake.

The longer we are in ministry, the more we appreciate how God chooses to influence people with the gospel through the lives of all kinds of people. As a pastor, I (Brian) am learning that it is the people, not necessarily the pastors, that go out into the global market place every day carrying the light of Christ into a darkened culture in need of hope. What's ironic is that it is not the kind of job or how much money a person makes that determines her influence for Christ. It is merely her identity in Christ as she is faithful to occupy the place of influence He chooses to give her. So nurturing that identity is important.

Begin by helping your kids identify their personal interests, talents, and spiritual gifts. What do you notice about your teenager that you can cultivate with encouragement? Is she compassionate toward people? Does she have a natural affinity for teaching? Is she a leader? Does she demonstrate courage under pressure? Is she a servant? As you begin to see patterns and characteristics emerge, encourage these in your teenager. Have real conversation about life after high school. Explore with them potential points of influence in the world. Remember, influence for the Kingdom's sake is based on identity in Christ, not in worldly success. Help her pursue the dream that God has put on her heart whether that is to be an astronaut, a teacher, a mom, or a police officer.

Give your teenager the vision for becoming a game changer in the world for the cause of Christ. It's one thing to cultivate his vision to be an astronaut. It is quite another thing to help him see that being an astronaut can never be his core identity or purpose. These things are only found in Christ. Becoming an astronaut, or a teacher, or a businessperson is merely a place of influence for the sake of the gospel. Perhaps the best way to give teens this kind of vision is to help them interact with people who are living for Christ in their area of interest. Be intentional in this regard. One of our daughters is expressing a lot of interests in teaching. We are super intentional about letting her get to know teachers that are impacting lives for Jesus Christ in their classrooms. We want our kids to see the vision in action and imagine themselves in that place of influence as a light in the world. One of our teenagers is expressing an interest in nursing. We have surrounded her with three medical professionals that are living for Christ as a light while they care for people every day. This visible demonstration of the vision inspires, motivates, and encourages kids toward expressing their identity in Christ in the ways He designed them for Kingdom purposes.

If you can help them see how their identity in Christ dictates their mission, and how their God-called assignment trumps everything, then they will light the world with the gospel of Jesus Christ. What is the mission of someone whose identity is in Jesus Christ? Jesus said this to all of His disciples. "Go therefore and make disciples of all nations, baptizing them in the name of the Father and of the Son and of the Holy Spirit, teaching them to observe all that I have commanded you. And behold, I am with you always, to the end of the age."[8] Give them vision to be whatever God has wired them to be so they can light the world in their generation for the glory of Christ.

When Attitudes and Actions Do Not Match Identity

There is an equally real, less exciting, other side of nurturing your teenager's identity in Christ. It is true that one's identity in Christ should influence every thought, every spoken word, every decision, every relationship, and every motive. It is also true that our teenager's attitudes and actions are not always in line with their identity in Christ. So what are we supposed to do when their attitudes and actions do not match their identity in Christ?

In our ministry we have counseled hundreds of parents whose teenagers did something "unbecoming of a Christian." Usually, by the time they get to us the parents are exasperated. We usually start by asking something like, "How have you parented through this, thus far?" We get all kinds of answers to that question. Things like, "We haven't done anything yet" or "We don't know what to do." Then there is the other extreme. "Well Pastor, we are having our daughter copy the book of Leviticus in English and Hebrew so she really understands the law" or "Right now, we make our son memorize two passages of Scripture per day on purity and this week he will attend our small group and confess his sins publically to the adults in our group." You think we are joking.

Truly, as parents of teenagers ourselves, we have been in the "We don't know what to do" category several times. Just like many rookie parents of teenagers, we have been shocked from time to time when our teenaged children exhibit qualities or behavior that are not rooted in their true identity in Christ. We have learned some things that are effective and that we were blind to initially. Foundationally, we need to understand that our teenagers are in a battle on two fronts for their identity. First, teenagers battle their flesh just like we do. The only difference is that they have less experience fighting that battle. Sometimes they will lose the battle. Second, our teenagers are in a spiritual battle for their identity in Christ. Sometimes our kids face external spiritual forces using temptation and torment as their weapons of choice. This is a very real battle reminiscent of the Apostle

Paul's words in Ephesians 6:12. "For we do not wrestle against flesh and blood, but against the rulers, against the authorities, against the cosmic powers over this present darkness, against the spiritual forces of evil in the heavenly places."[9] Understanding this will change our methodology when our teenagers exhibit behavior contrary to their identity in Christ. As parents we need to fight spiritual battles in the proper spiritual ways. Without writing you a prescription, here is our process.

1. *Pray.*

Often, when we encounter attitudes and behavior that is disappointing, we react. For us, reactive parenting never goes well. We have tried it. Instead of reacting, buy yourself some time and pray. There is some help you need in order to parent in the midst of a spiritual battle. Make time to pray for wisdom from the Holy Spirit. What is really going on in your teenager's heart may not be perfectly clear in the beginning. You may have partial information. They may not be ready or able to talk about the problems. They may not even know exactly why they are feeling certain ways causing abnormal behavior. Often we need clarity from the Lord to understand. Also ask the Holy Spirit to give you counsel. If the battle is spiritual, who better to provide you insight into the situation than God Himself? If that seems like a foreign concept to you maybe a simple, hypothetical, example will help.

You begin to feel constant disrespect from your teenaged son. At first you blow it off as "hormonal." Then, you begin to sense that something else is going on. His anger seems to be through the roof. He yells at you and walks away from you in disrespect. He seems angry all the time. One night, in a fit of rage, he punches a hole in the sheetrock wall of his bedroom. You are livid first and then deeply concerned. This disrespect and anger is out of control. Where is it coming from? You engage your son with a series of questions and frustrated statements. "Why are you so angry?" "You have a great life and a great family. Why are you treating us this way?" You get the typical response. His head is down. His eyes are on the floor. "I don't know," he says. "Well that doesn't help," you think to yourself in frustration. Baffled, you walk away to pray. "Lord, I love him. I know you love him. I know he loves you, but he's not in a good place right now. He has forgotten he is your child. He doesn't have your peace. He's angry, Father. What is making him so angry? Help me, Lord. Give me counsel that comes from you. Give me wisdom to see what I can't see. Amen." As you are pacing the floor trying to decide what to do a thought hits you. He started taking a new medication a few months ago, so you frantically look for the packaging and label that lists all of the potential side effects. As you read, everything begins to make sense. "This medication may cause mood swings, anger episodes, or abnormal bouts of depression." While this may not be all of the issue, you realize instantly that it is a contributor. How did you know to check the side effects of the new medication? When we pray, God gives us wisdom that comes from outside of ourselves. It may sound ethereal or miraculous or even crazy to you, but it's true. We need help from God to parent our teens when their attitudes and actions do not match their identity in Christ.

2. Connect with your baby.

Remember that this teenager, who may be causing pain or hurt or anger in your life at the moment, is still your baby. It is not as if "the alien moved in" at age twelve and they are somehow a different person, excusable by their season of adolescence. He is your baby. Love him like you did when he cried after falling down or got angry when someone took a toy away from him. After you pray, connect with your teenager emotionally. Slow everything down. Sit down. Ask him to sit down with you. Ask him questions. This prevents you from making assumptions that may not be accurate. Begin with open-ended questions. "I have noticed that you seem really angry lately. Is everything OK?" Even if they don't answer you right away, you have given them the opportunity to share their story. That may seem like it does not matter in the moment, but in the long run it certainly will.

3. *Confront the sin.*

Once you have sought wisdom from God and connected with your teenager to hear his story, it is time to confront. Some parents avoid confrontation at all cost, but this is a mistake. In a calm and wise manner, confront the attitude or behavior for the purpose of shaping heart and identity. Our worst moments as parents are when we lose our temper at the point of confrontation. Proper confrontation highlights the offending attitude or behavior. It also clarifies expectations for the actions of your teenager in the future. Always, in confrontation, we are praying for our teenager to have a humble spirit demonstrated in words and actions of repentance, reconciliation, and forgiveness. It does not always happen that way, right away. However, a teenager who is also a disciple of Jesus will surely bend to the grace-based conviction of the Holy Spirit eventually.

4. *Release the tribe.*

We have found that parenting teenagers requires a tribe. Our tribe consists of people that also genuinely care about and invest in our children regularly. We quickly reach out to a small group leader, a youth pastor, a teacher, a coach, and a friend who is a counselor if our teenagers seem to be going through something that doesn't quite match their identity in Christ. These kinds of people are very important in shaping your child's identity in Christ, especially in times that seem fairly volatile for their well-being. Some parents are afraid to involve others. We find that we need the community of faith to help us parent our teenagers. When you are in a difficult season, inform the tribe. Release them to keep their eyes open, lean into your child's life, and echo truth in love that you are sharing at home. It is interesting. There are times a 26-year-old small group leader can say the exact same thing you are saying but with radically different results. Don't be afraid to release the tribe.

5. *Pray more specifically.*

When your teen's attitudes and actions betray their identity in Christ, you will learn to pray more specifically and in strategic ways. This will be a relentless effort. This time you are praying with the wisdom God has given you concerning your teenager. Maybe you have discovered that they struggle with lust or that they have a tendency toward depression. Now you can pray for them in very specific ways. This kind of prayer wages war against the enemy by the power of the Holy Spirit for your teenager's identity in Christ. Prayer like this is powerful. It is completely dependent on God for ongoing freedom and peace in your teenager's life because of Christ. Pray, pray, and pray some more. This is the work of relentless parenting.

Building your teenager's identity in Christ is not your job alone. If it were, it would be overwhelming. Be encouraged. God does His part. In Christ your teenager is His child. He will work by His Spirit and through His Word to slowly shape her into the person He desires her to become for His glory. He will use the community of faith—the church—to partner with you to lead your kids to their place of influence. In time they will become like a city set on a hill that others turn to for light in the dark of night. It won't be because of what they do, it will be because of who they are as disciples of Jesus.

Endnotes

[1] Vern L. Bengston, *Families and Faith: How Religion is Passed Down Across the Generations* (Oxford University Press, 2013), 185-186.
[2] Genesis 1:26-28 (ESV)
[3] Ephesians 2:1-3 (ESV)
[4] Romans 5:10 (ESV)
[5] Ephesians 2:4-7 (ESV)
[6] 1 John 4:10 (ESV)
[7] Matthew 5:14-16 (ESV)
[8] Matthew 28:19-20 (ESV)
[9] Ephesians 6:12 (ESV)

Chapter 9

Freedom to Parent Relentlessly

When we read parenting books we always walk away with a list of things we should be doing that we are not, and it can feel exasperating or even exhausting. We have learned to ask God for one take away that we can implement. Hopefully as you finish this book you are simply thinking to yourself, "I need to pursue my teenager's heart, relentlessly." That requires a normal and consistent demonstration of love no matter the circumstances. This demonstration of love can be difficult for parents because we wonder if we know how to love relentlessly. We feel love for our child but we balk sometimes, because we feel inadequate, or hypocritical, fearful, or even deeply wounded. It is precisely this "hesitation" that distances us from our teenagers. It eventually renders our relationship mediocre and our influence negligible. Why do we hesitate?

When you and I come to family life, we bring along things that affect the family dynamic and the formation of each person in the home. These "things" can be positive or negative. Positively we may bring an easily demonstrated sense of compassion because our parents knew how to show us compassion. Or, maybe you are healthy emotionally, physically, and spiritually and you properly contribute to the health of your teenager. Maybe you know what it means to be obedient and walk with God, thus demonstrating this in authenticity.

It is the negative issues that cause us to hesitate though, as we seek to demonstrate love properly in the pursuit of our teenager's heart. Some of these things are obvious to everyone. Other issues are secret or hidden, yet the effects are potent. These "things" can be rooted in personal sin, past or present, or in wounds caused by the sins of others against us. Often these sins give birth to issues that manifest like anger, depression, shame, or detachment. Anger repels our teenagers. Depression or detachment distances us from our teenagers. Shame keeps us from dealing with our teenagers around issues we cannot master ourselves, giving birth to blame. In the crucial pursuit of our teenager's heart, these strongholds keep us from parenting relentlessly and cause hesitation. From these "things" we need healing and freedom for our own wellbeing and for the journey of parenting teenagers.

Strongholds

What are these "things" that seem to hold us captive and cause us to hesitate in the loving pursuit of our child's heart? In order to answer that question, we need to agree on a few truths that we don't usually consider, when it comes to parenting. From the moment of conception, God has been working His spiritual purposes for your life through Christ with singular intent, that you may have life and have it abundantly according to John 10:10. This includes, but is not limited to, your salvation and your spiritual wellbeing that will yield both temporal and eternal blessings. Equally true is the fact that a less powerful and defeated enemy, has been working with opposite intent. He is at work to kill, steal, and destroy your life and consequently the lives of those that you love most—including your teenaged son or daughter. Though Christ is the Victor and the battle is won, we as humans have a propensity to believe lies. Satan knows this and since you were very young, he has been telling you lies, effectively and consistently. In certain moments of your life, if you are like most, you listened. You believe something about yourself or about God that was not true. A strong-hold is "anything we know to be against the will of God, which we also see as unchangeable."[1] It is a faulty belief system that allows our experience and false beliefs to overshadow the truth of God's Word. Strongholds are spiritual but they impact spirit, soul, and body; we cannot just wish them away. In case you are still uncertain about what a stronghold is, let us give you a few examples that may help clarify so you might recognize them in your own life.

Fear is a common stronghold. Rejection is another. Pride, shame, unbelief, lust, various addictions, unforgiving attitudes, depression, anger, and constant regret, all are very common strongholds. Add to these, traumatic wounds emotionally or spiritually, judgments we have made against ourselves, God, or another, and certain vows we have taken based on lies, and you have a list of the most common strongholds in the lives of people, exposing the enemy's bag of tricks. So how do these strongholds form in our lives?

ANATOMY OF A STRONGHOLD

Examples: Fear, Rejection, Pride, Shame, Unbelief, Lust, Addictions, Unforgiveness, Depression, Anger, Regret, Soul Ties, Vows/Judgments, Trauma, etc.

PAIN

EVENT

FEAR

OTHERS REACT

Idolatry
1. Source of Truth?
2. Source of Security?
3. Source of comfort?

LIE

Answer?
Repent = Change Sources

DEFENSE COMFORT

Hear God
1. How do I defend self?
2. How do I seek comfort?
3. Confess/Receive
4. Renounce way & role
5. Invite the Father to be your source
6. Agree/Confess

Hear God
1. What is the lie?
2. Confess/Receive
3. Renounce the lie.
4. Forgive?
5. What's the truth?
6. Agree/Confess

Typically, a stronghold begins with an event in our lives that is significant in every way. The event may be traumatic such as a form of abuse. We once counseled a parent—let's call her Amy—who was full of fear especially as it related to her teenager going on mission trips supervised by vetted and qualified adults in the church. As we learned more, it became clear that her fear stemmed from an event from her childhood. An extended family member, whom she trusted, sexually abused her while she was under his care. This event that occurred around age eight, triggered fear that impacted her in many ways through her forties, including how she parented her teenagers.

The event could also be less obvious. Something like the way a person in authority responded to you when you shared your feelings. We ministered to a parent, Tim, struggling with perfectionism and superimposing that perfectionism on his very imperfect teenagers. As we began to pray through the root of the perfectionism he recalled an event that occurred as an elementary student. After working methodically to color a picture as an assignment for his class, the teacher walked by and pointed out the one tiny area where he "colored outside the lines." There was no positive affirmation for his work. This was catalytic for his stronghold of perfectionism and that stronghold was wreaking havoc in his family.

We worked with another well-intended father named Jeff. When Jeff was around ten years old, he and a group of neighborhood friends built a fort in the woods behind his neighborhood. It was an awesome place to escape. The fort was on the side of a hill with a stream below. For Jeff it was like he had stepped into another world. He said that he often took his bow and arrow or pellet gun and disappeared for hours. One day when he arrived at the fort, he went in and one of the other guys had left behind a pornographic magazine as a gift for the preteen band of brothers. This was an event that forged a stronghold of lust. As a father of a teen daughter, this stronghold gave birth to unhealthy fears in Jeff's parenting.

Whatever the event, it is unique to you. In ways, these events are like snow flakes. They are unique and different from person to person as if they were uniquely orchestrated to cause a person to wrestle with very "common to humanity" strongholds throughout their lives. These are such destructive schemes of Satan.

These events most often cause pain and fear. The Bible teaches us in Galatians 5:22-23, that the fruit of the Holy Spirit is love, joy, peace, patience, kindness, goodness, faithfulness, gentleness, and self-control. Not fear or pain though. The Bible also teaches us in 2 Timothy 1:7 that God did not give us a spirit of fear but instead one of power and love and self-control. Then, looking through the lens of Scripture, it is also true that pain and fear caused by the strongholds in our lives are the fruit of another spirit; a satanic spirit. Recognizing this is important because it allows us to see evidence in our own lives of the spiritual battle that every human is engaged in whether they know it or not. The apostle Paul tells believers in Ephesians 6:12 that "We do not wrestle against flesh and blood but against rulers, authorities, against the cosmic powers over this present darkness, against the spiritual forces of evil in the heavenly places." Strongholds in your life have been planned as part of the spiritual battle for your soul and for the generations that stem from your family. This may be uncomfortable to think about, but it is biblically true.

It is possible that you already know the event in your life that launched a present stronghold. Maybe as you have been reading, God has brought that event to your mind with crystal clarity. That's good! We need to identify the event in order to break the stronghold. Often, though, we suppress these events and forget. This is how we protect ourselves emotionally. It is in this case that we need to ask the Holy Spirit to shed light on the situation. We need to know the truth.

As a stronghold takes root, the catalytic event gives birth to a lie. When an event causing pain and fear like this occurs, especially in our childhood, we are very susceptible to believing lies. Because we are hurting or fearful, we are hyper-attune to spiritual influences in these moments. So the enemy takes the opportunity to whisper lies. For Amy, who had a stronghold of fear forged through abuse, the lie she believed was, "I cannot trust anyone." She even made a vow to go with the lie. "I will never trust another man again." While completely understandable, this lie and subsequent vow of her past began tragically impacting the present lives of her teenagers who were not allowed to experience any group event led by men. The event gave birth to a lie that was now seeping into the next generation of her family. She was teaching her teenagers that they couldn't trust any man. That's a problem when the Bible repeatedly teaches us to address God as "Father" and the only way to Him is by trusting the man, Christ Jesus. Satan is pretty crafty, isn't he?

Tim, the perfectionistic father, believed a terrible lie. He believed that unless he did everything perfectly, he was not valuable. Therefore, he constantly felt paranoid and worthless. As a parent of teenagers, he demanded perfection from his kids as a result of the lie he believed, driving a wedge between himself and his teenagers. His stronghold kept him from pursuing his teenagers' hearts and held him captive to feelings of worthlessness.

Jeff, who had been a lustful preteen believed that every teen had dark secrets. His irrational fears and issues with over protection caused him to distrust his sons even though his teenagers were trustworthy. In Jeff's efforts to protect, he actually created a chasm between his heart and that of his teen children. The stronghold plus the lie gave birth to fear, counteracting Jeff's desire to pursue the heart of his teen. Instead it formed a relational gap and emotional walls. This stronghold actually breeds contempt since Jeff tells them that their Father God is constantly looking to bust them. That's very different than a loving Father who knew their sin and paid the price with His own blood to forgive that sin. The enemy uses strongholds in one generation to distort the love of God and the truth of the gospel for the next generation.

The thing about a stronghold is that it continues to cause pain and fear throughout life unless it is broken. It is cyclical in a way. Whenever we experience pain or fear we attempt to defend ourselves or to comfort ourselves. A stronghold will often dictate how we defend ourselves and to what or whom we go to for comfort. Turning to anything or anyone but God for our defense is blatant idolatry although it may seem subtle. This is Satan's goal for you. Idolatry. People medicate pain or protect themselves from feelings of pain in so many ways. We turn to various kinds of idols, from people to pornography. In our case studies, Amy isolated herself, and consequently her kids, in fear when it was time to defend or protect. This isolation caused detachment and feelings of depression for Amy. For her teenagers, Amy's tendency to isolate and protect them caused frustration and feelings of resentment from the teenager toward the parent. Tim, the perfectionist, defended and protected himself in times of pain or fear by becoming hyper-controlling. Even worse, when he could no longer control his situation or circumstances, he drank alcohol to escape. This stronghold caused his teenagers to lose respect for him and resent him because of his downward spiral when things weren't perfect. Jeff jumped right back into pornography when he needed to find escape from pain or fear. This secret stronghold built a chasm between him and his children that everyone could sense but no one could identify or clearly articulate. It also left Jeff full of shame and anger, negatively impacting his heart connection with his teenagers. When there is a stronghold in a parent's life, the behavior associated with defending and comforting oneself in times of fear or pain always causes others to react. How others react often will reinforce the stronghold with a new event and the whole cycle starts over again, giving birth to full-blown dysfunction in the family and hijacking any chance we as parents have to effectively pursue the hearts of our children.

Generational Sin

Identifying and dealing with personal strongholds in our lives as parents is very important. It is crucial on two fronts in the spiritual battle for your life and family. First, it is important to break free for the wellbeing of your soul and the trajectory of your life. Our strongholds hold us captive to ways of living that hinder our sense of peace and wellbeing and our experience with God. This is primary because breaking free from our strongholds changes us and fills us with things like hope, joy, and peace. This change sets us up to be the best we can be as relentless parents. There is another reason that we must fight for personal freedom. Our strongholds and the associated sin patterns can be passed down to the next generation. A generational sin is an unholy influence or tendency in a family lineage to accept as normal or excusable something that controls the behavior of many in the family. Think about it and you will instantly recognize that this is true. A father that commits serial adultery is likely to raise a son or a daughter that also commits adultery. A physically abusive parent is likely to raise a child who becomes a parent who is also physically abusive. We know from marriage counseling to always ask an engaged couple about the marriages of their parents. Why? Parents who have remained in a committed relationship with the same marriage partner throughout life are much more likely to raise children who also stay committed in their marriage relationships. The inverse is also true. These are common and obvious examples but generational sin is multifaceted in its forms and levels of brokenness. The important concept for us to recognize as relentless parents is that sin is transferrable from one generation to the next. For the love of God and our children, we must be willing to identify the strongholds in our lives and break free.

Breaking Free from Strongholds

The good news is that Jesus came to set us free from these strongholds. In Isaiah 61:1 the prophet indicates that hundreds of years before the birth of Christ, he (Jesus) would come to set the captives free. "The Spirit of the Lord God is upon me, because the LORD has anointed me to bring good news to the poor; he has sent me to bind up the brokenhearted, to proclaim liberty to the captives, and the opening of the prison to those who are bound."[2] This is really good news. As a believer in Christ, you and I were not meant to live captive to strongholds. Instead, Christ has come to set us free and mend our broken hearts. Many people, even Christians, who are captive to strongholds, tell themselves there is no hope. They feel as if the stronghold is too strong to be broken. Jesus is greater. He is more powerful and He is the one who can free you. We're also reminded in Scripture that, "If the Son sets you free, you will be free indeed."[3] So breaking free requires faith in the one who can set you free—Jesus.

Breaking away from strongholds requires the work of the Spirit through the truth of God's Word all wrapped in the faith that Jesus can set you free by His blood. Since these strongholds are spiritual and formed in a spiritual battle, they must be broken spiritually. While psychology provides knowledge based on human observation, it is not enough to break a stronghold. Freedom from bondage comes as a work of the Holy Spirit. Galatians 3:13-14 says that, "Christ redeemed us from the curse of the law by becoming a curse for us—for it is written, 'Cursed is everyone who is hanged on a tree'—so that in Christ Jesus the blessing of Abraham might come to the Gentiles, so that we might receive the promised Spirit through faith."[4] Latch on to an important truth here. For every person that is experiencing the curse of sin (including strongholds) Jesus became curse for us by His own crucifixion. In this selfless act of grace toward His creation, Jesus appeased the justice of God and effectively broke the stronghold of sin for every person who would believe. In this way He made all who would confess Him as Lord free from the law of sin and death and victorious spiritually. The good news is we never have to be captive to sin again, though we can walk back into it. "For freedom Christ has set us free;

stand firm therefore, and do not submit again to a yoke of slavery," as shown in Galatians 5:1. Through the power of the Holy Spirit we can walk in a new way because of Christ, free of sin. In Galatians 5:16-17 Paul implores believers to be free from strongholds of the flesh. "But I say, walk by the Spirit, and you will not gratify the desires of the flesh. For the desires of the flesh are against the Spirit, and the desires of the Spirit are against the flesh, for these are opposed to each other, to keep you from doing the things you want to do." When we seek freedom we find it only in walking by the Spirit. How would we go about such a journey?

We begin by praying for wisdom about these strongholds. Even if you have read this chapter and thought to yourself, "I don't have any strongholds," continue to pray and ask God to reveal anything that might be hidden or any root of sin or disbelief that is now so normal that you do not even perceive it. This will require listening to the Holy Spirit. Our experience is that when we ask God to reveal anything in our lives that is harming us, our family, or the generations that will come—He is faithful to speak to us. Distinguishing the voice of the Holy Spirit is really not complicated. What the Holy Spirit says will never contradict Scripture and will always expose things that are hidden as if shining light in the darkness. Often, when we pray and ask God to reveal these strongholds, he speaks to us in our "gut" for lack of a better term. Our job is to write down what the Holy Spirit is saying to us and check it against the Word of God to make sure we are hearing His voice.

Take a Cross Trip

The path to freedom is to the cross through prayer. When it is time to pursue freedom, it is important to find a quiet place to be alone with God. Take your Bible and journal, and then isolate yourself. If you are fearful, ask a trusted friend to pray for you while you are seeking God for freedom from strongholds. You might even ask another believer to be with you while you are praying, or to sit outside your room, office, or closet while you are praying—specifically to intercede for you in prayer.

Begin by praising God in worship. This allows you to align your heart with His. It squarely places you in a humble and submissive posture and exalts the Father as the one who is able to break every stronghold and free us from every sin. Once you have praised, you may then pray through the anatomy of a stronghold diagram. Here is a four-step prayer guide to show you how.

1. *Pray and ask the Holy Spirit to reveal any event in your past that was the beginning or the root of the stronghold in your life.*

Ask Him for ears to hear His voice and a heart that is open to His Spirit. As the Holy Spirit brings an event or series of events to mind, open your journal, and write these things down. This may take some time. Write down everything you can remember about the event with as much clarity as the Holy Spirit gives you. Then, describe the pain or fear that you felt associated with that event. Write down what caused you pain or what bred fear in you concerning this event. Be as specific as possible.

2. *Pray and ask God to expose any lie that you believed about Him, yourself, or others that tightened the grip of a stronghold in your life.*

Ask Him, "What is the lie?" Listen. What does the Holy Spirit reveal to you in your spirit? Often God will reveal a version of one of seven core lies. I am incompetent, unworthy, unacceptable, un-loveable, disconnected, imperfect, or powerless. As the Holy Spirit exposes the lie or lies, write these down specifically.

3. *Ask the Lord to help you deal with the lies head on.*

As you understand the lies you have believed, confess this to God and seek His forgiveness. You may pray something like,

"I realize now that I believed I had to be perfect to be valued. This is a lie. Forgive me for believing that perfection is the requirement for Your love and to be accepted by others." Then, renounce the lie and replace it with truth. "Lord, I renounce the lie of perfectionism in my life. Instead, I choose to believe the truth that no one is perfect, but by your grace You have loved me and made me righteous by the work of Your shed blood on the cross." "Your word is truth and it says there is not one perfect, not even one. Your Word tells me that while I was still sinning, still imperfect, You died for me because You loved me and wanted me to be free." "Your Word tells me that I can't ever do enough to earn Your love. Instead, You choose to love me not because I am perfect but because I am Your creation." Write all of this in your journal and as you are praying, verbalize your prayers aloud. The enemy will lie to you again later and tell you that all of this was in your head.

4. *Ask the Holy Spirit to show you any idolatrous ways in which you seek defense and comfort as you face pain and fear.*

Pray and ask, "Lord, show me how I defend myself and seek comfort in ways that are not of You." As the Lord reveals these ways to you, write them in your journal. Repent of these ways as they are revealed to you. "Lord forgive me for turning to alcohol, pornography, or another person in an unhealthy way (you fill in the blank) when I need defense or comfort. I renounce that way now in Jesus' name and I invite You to be my source of defense and comfort. Be my defender, God. Be my comfort, my Father, in Jesus' name." As you repent, you are leaving behind your old source and turning to God. In this spiritual act of prayer, you are crushing the idols in your life and turning to God, the only true Defender and Comforter. Again, write all of this down. Verbalize your prayers aloud. Believe God for freedom. He will set you free indeed.

Though just a primer on finding freedom from strongholds, this prayer process will lead you to a new level of freedom in Christ. Will you ever be tempted again regarding the forms of idolatry prevalent in your life? You probably will but because you are free you will recognize the trap and you can fight that temptation with truth, through the Holy Spirit, in prayer. Make it a discipline to take frequent cross trips to align your heart, mind, and soul with God in prayer turning to Him as your perfect source of defense and comfort.

Fight for Freedom for your Teen

As you receive freedom from strongholds in your own life your spiritual eyes as a parent will more easily identify strongholds in your teenager's life. You may recognize these strongholds as eerily familiar since you passed them on as generational sin. Their strongholds may be unique because of events they have experienced hidden from you and unique to them personally. Whatever the source of the strongholds in the lives of our teenagers, as we recognize them, we must fight relentlessly for the spiritual freedom of our teenager. This fight takes place in prayer. The process is the same as when we are seeking freedom for our own strongholds. This time we are taking a cross trip on behalf of our child. Use the same four steps, same procedure, and same anatomy of a stronghold. The only difference is that we are asking God to reveal what is hidden in our kids' lives so we can pray against the strongholds in Jesus' name. In this way we are interceding for them, and fighting for them spiritually. We pray for God to illuminate the lies that they have believed so we can help them. We ask God to reveal to them the lies that they believe. We ask the Holy Spirit to crush the idols in their lives and to draw them to Christ as their source of defense and comfort. We beg God to reveal to them their bondage and bring them freedom in Christ. This is a relentless prayer effort. As parents of teenagers, we have realized that the only way to fight a spiritual battle is through prayer. Whether it's pornography, perfectionism, or some other stronghold, our teenagers are susceptible, and in fact the enemy is planning to create strongholds in their lives. Who else will intercede for them if not us? Most parents don't know to fight for their teenagers in prayer this way. Most teenagers do not even know what a stronghold is. Regardless, fight for them in prayer. Teach them about strongholds and idolatry. Show them how to pray this way. This is a spiritual battle and freedom is experienced through the work of the Holy Spirit.

A Girl Named Hazel

Once upon a time, there was a little girl named Hazel. She was a very sad little girl. Hazel had one sister named Daisy who was very much loved—actually favored—by her mother. Sadly, Hazel was disliked and emotionally neglected by her mother. For many years, Hazel tried and tried to receive love and affection from her mom, without success.

Then one day, some hope entered Hazel's life. Her paternal grandmother had to move in with the family and share a room and bed with sad little Hazel. As it turned out, Hazel's grandmother was a confessed Christian. Sharing so much time together allowed Hazel to receive the love and compassion from her grandmother that she had been lacking from her mother. Hazel began to learn about the love and sacrifice of Jesus Christ and how she was created to be with God, and was created for a purpose.

At the age of fifteen, Hazel met her prince charming, Cecil, at a community dance. She was soon given permission, by her father, to marry Cecil. He knew that she would live a happier life being married, even at the age of fifteen. Cecil, her prince charming, also loved the Lord and began to demonstrate the love of Christ to Hazel. Hazel's life changed and she slowly overcame her very sad circumstances because of her new identity in Christ and the freedom from the past found in the Lord.

Eleven years later, Hazel gave birth to a daughter (and later a son) becoming a mother herself. She loved and cherished her children, Mabel and Cecil, Jr., very much. Her motherhood, because of Christ, was very different than that of her abusive mother. Hazel spent her lifetime sharing and showing the love of Christ to her children, grandchildren, and great-grandchildren. I (Angela) am one of those grandchildren who became part of this Christian heritage so lovingly and diligently passed on by my mother. And now my children, Hailey, Madelyn, and Eden, are some of Hazel's great-grandchildren whom I have the gift and privilege to intentionally teach the truth and love of Christ. Thank You, God, for the gift of faith and freedom that You provided Hazel so many years ago. For when Hazel found freedom in Christ from the abuse of her past, it changed everything in our family. What could have been anger and abuse became love and legacy.

One Person's Freedom Changes Everything

Finding freedom to parent relentlessly is worth it. Hazel is an example from our family of how an abused daughter became a pillar of faith yielding a legacy of freedom in Christ. How could your personal freedom from strongholds change everything for your children, grandchildren, and great-grandchildren? Though the story is yet to be written, we know, one person's freedom in the family tree changes everything. The fight is worth it and the battle is the Lord's. When we turn to Him, faithfully, He sets the captives free.

Endnotes

[1] Gateway Church, Kairos: When Eternity Steps into Time. Pg. 2, 2013.
[2] Isaiah 61:1 (ESV)
[3] John 8:36 (ESV)
[4] Galatians 3:13-14 (ESV)
[5] Galatians 5:26-17 (ESV)

Final Thoughts

"Relentless" is an interesting word. It could be used in a negative way to describe a "helicopter" parent. You know, the kind of parent that is always hovering in every aspect of their teenager's life. Relentless could describe the "boa constrictor" parent. That's the parent who is constantly tightening their grip in fear that they will lose control. Neither of these are what we mean when we use the phrase "relentless parenting."

Relentless parenting is based on a core value of relentless love. The kind of love that never stops, never wavers, never is cut off. It is an insistent affection full of selflessness and sacrifice and doing the hard things. Relentless parenting is pursuing the heart of your teenager even when he decides he will not demonstrate love for you in return. It is an unrelenting pursuit, but it is healthy, not stifling. Relentless parenting is not codependent or controlling. The crucial pursuit of your teen's heart is characterized by leadership, love, and the upholding of truth. To love and parent relentlessly requires wisdom and grace that only come from God.

Think about the way Jesus loves us. Consider how God persistently loves and leads His children. He is consistent, extravagant, miraculous and routine all at the same time. He is a Perfect Father shepherding us toward grace and truth. This is our model, and He is our source. We need wisdom, patience, truth, grace, love, and peace in order to parent relentlessly during the teen years. Let us encourage you not to go it alone in this journey. Though some days are difficult, we also experience joy in this journey of parenting teenagers. The joy comes from our source—Jesus. When with think about doing anything significant, especially with spiritual ramifications, we know we can't go it alone. Jesus makes that clear even to His disciples in John 15:5 "I am the vine; you are the branches. Whoever abides in me and I in him, he it is that bears much fruit for apart from me you can do nothing."[1] Relentless parenting means insistently abiding in Christ. We need Him to parent our teens and to lovingly pursue them daily. Stay connected to Him. Don't try this alone. You will find joy, hope, and wisdom while abiding with Christ and resting in His power beyond yourself.

Every day is important in this journey. Most days in your life are ordinary, normal, and even mundane to a degree. It is precisely in the typical days of life that we do our best relentless parenting. Deuteronomy 6:4-7 says, "Here, O Israel: The LORD our God, the LORD is one. You shall love the LORD your God with all your heart and with all your soul and with all your might. And these words that I command you today shall be on your heart. You shall teach them diligently to your children, and shall talk of them when you sit in your house, and when you walk by the way, and when you lie down, and when you rise."[2] That's the plan. Every day in the ordinary moments, we are relentless. And, as parents of teenagers, we pursue the heart of the teen. It's crucial for them, for you, for the expanding Kingdom of Jesus, and for a legacy of faith in Christ rippling into the generations. Grace and peace, friends.

Endnotes

[1] John 15:5 (ESV)
[2] Dt. 6:4-7 (ESV)

MORE FAMILY RESOURCES
from Randall House

52 Creative Family Time Experiences

TIMOTHY SMITH

Connecting Church and Home

DR. TIM KIMMEL

The Legacy Path

BRIAN HAYNES

Tech Savvy Parenting

BRIAN HOUSMAN

Practical Family Ministry

TIMOTHY PAUL JONES AND JOHN DAVID TRENTHAM

Five Reasons for Spiritual Apathy in Teens

ROB AND AMY RIENOW

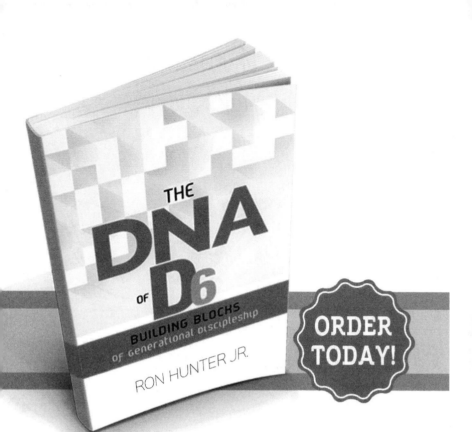

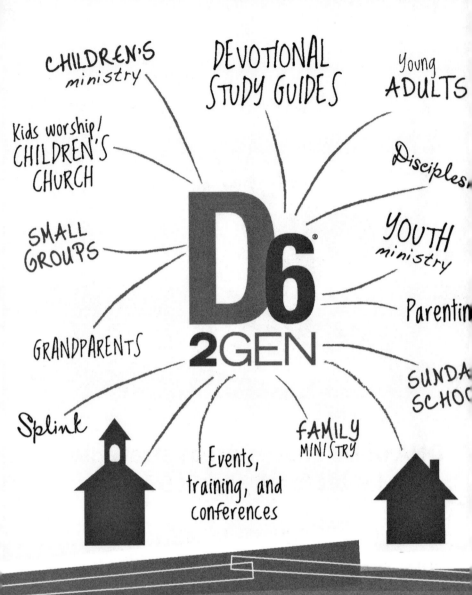

CHILDREN'S ministry

DEVOTIONAL STUDY GUIDES

young ADULTS

Kids worship/ CHILDREN'S CHURCH

Disciples

SMALL GROUPS

YOUTH ministry

Parentin

GRANDPARENTS

D6 2GEN

SUNDA SCHOO

Splink

Events, training, and conferences

FAMILY MINISTRY

A FAMILY-ALIGNED CURRICULUM FOR EVERY GENERATION.

WWW.D62GEN.COM

Based on Deuteronomy 6:5-7